Papers of the Medieval Hispanic Research Seminar 67

Publications of the Magdalen Iberian Medieval Studies Seminar 1

RAMÓN MENÉNDEZ PIDAL AFTER FORTY YEARS: A REASSESSMENT

Papers of the Medieval Hispanic Research Seminar

Menéndez Pidal in Oxford, 28 June 1922.

RAMÓN MENÉNDEZ PIDAL AFTER FORTY YEARS: A REASSESSMENT

Edited by

JUAN-CARLOS CONDE

Department of Hispanic Studies
Queen Mary, University of London

2010

In memoriam
DIEGO CATALÁN
(1928–2008)

&

ALAN DEYERMOND
(1932–2009)

The PMHRS logo on the half-title is from
the *Cancionero d'Herberay des Essarts*, redrawn by Martin J. Ryan.

Typeset by David Barnett using XɴTEX
Printed and bound by The Bidnall Press

© Department of Hispanic Studies,
Queen Mary and Westfield College, London, 2010

ISBN 0 902238 71 x
ISSN 1460-051X

Contents

Abbreviations

BH	*Bulletin Hispanique*
BHS	*Bulletin of Hispanic Studies*
BRAH	*Boletín de la Real Academia de la Historia*
C	*La Corónica*
CCa	Clásicos Castalia
CSIC	Consejo Superior de Investigaciones Científicas
FCHE	Fuentes Cronísticas de la Historia de España
FRMP	Fundación Ramón Menéndez Pidal
HR	*Hispanic Review*
HSMS	Hispanic Seminary of Medieval Studies
MA	*Medium Aevum*
MHRA	Modern Humanities Research Association
NBAE	Nueva Biblioteca de Autores Españoles
NRFH	*Nueva Revista de Filología Hispánica*
PMHRS	Papers of the Medieval Hispanic Research Seminar
PMIMSS	Publications of the Magdalen Iberian Medieval Studies Seminar
RABM	*Revista de Archivos, Bibliotecas y Museos*
RAE	Real Academia Española
RFE	*Revista de Filología Española*
RPh	*Romance Philology*
SSMLL	Society for the Study of Medieval Languages and Literature

Ramón Menéndez Pidal and Oxford, Now and Then

JUAN-CARLOS CONDE
(*Magdalen College, University of Oxford & MIMSS*)

This volume contains the text of the papers presented at the conference *1968-2008: The work of Ramón Menéndez Pidal forty years after his death*, which took place on 30 May 2008 as part of the programme of activities of the newly created Magdalen Iberian Medieval Studies Seminar (MIMSS). As editor of this volume, and as founder and director of MIMSS, I should explain what the reasons were for revisiting Menéndez Pidal's work forty years after his death on 14 November 1968 — hence the title of this volume —, 112 years after the publication of his first book (Menéndez Pidal 1896) and, as I write these lines, 140 years and eleven days after his birth in La Coruña on 13 March 1869. I can say that, in addition to those provided by chronological factors, there are several good reasons to revisit Menéndez Pidal's contributions to the study of Hispanic culture.

The first reason has to do precisely with the vastness and diversity of Menéndez Pidal's scholarly enterprises. He published major works on literary, linguistic, historical, and philological issues; he dealt in his books and articles with different moments of Hispanic history, from the Middle Ages to the 20th century; and he examined this panoply of subjects and topics not only in Spain or Castile, but in the whole Hispanic world on both sides of the Atlantic. Even though his interests as a scholar were clearly focused on the Castilian Middle Ages, on the Spanish language and on Medieval Castilian literature, the wide breadth of Pidal's research interests is truly stunning and perfectly in line with what MIMSS, as a research seminar, wishes to achieve:

> [MIMSS] activities would include (but would not necessarily be restricted to) lectures, colloquia, workshops, conferences, seminars, and publications on Iberian medieval themes. These would include not only literary and linguistic topics [...], but also topics in history, music, art, religion, history of the

book, and other aspects of Iberian medieval culture. It is also important to underline that the Iberian scope that the MIMSS would adopt means that its activities would embrace not only the domain of Castilian language and culture, but also those of the Portuguese, Galician and Catalan languages and cultures. Aspects of the cultural developments associated with the Muslim presence in Medieval Iberia, as well as those connected with the Jewish minority that flourished in the Iberian Peninsula during the Middle Ages, would also be present in MIMSS' academic and research sessions. This ample array of interests and this wide scope almost automatically guarantee the interdisciplinary approach that all MIMSS activities would like to adopt (Conde 2007).

When in search of a subject for MIMSS' first colloquium which could properly embody the intended interdisciplinary character of the seminar, the idea of devoting it to a reassessment of Menéndez Pidal's work came to mind as almost inescapable: topics on linguistics, literature, history, historiography, oral literature and others could be examined and explored using Menéndez Pidal's contributions as a scholarly Ariadne's thread.

Another reason for considering that a reassessment of Menéndez Pidal's work was an interesting subject for a colloquium and for the subsequent volume of proceedings is provided by the intersection of two factors: the previous existence of other similar enterprises undertaken some years ago, the majority of them promoted, interestingly enough, outside Spain (see, for example, Deyermond 1992–93 and Hempel & Briesemeister 1982, produced respectively on the 25th and the 10th anniversaries of Menéndez Pidal's death); and the recent publication not only of major contributions to our knowledge of the life, work and intellectual heritage of Menéndez Pidal (see Pérez Villanueva 1991; Pérez Pascual 1998; Catalán 1992, 2001, 2005), but also of unpublished works by don Ramón himself, including his *La épica medieval española*, his long-awaited *Historia de la lengua española* and the *Glosario* which was supposed to be the second volume of *Orígenes del Español* (Menéndez Pidal 1992, Menéndez Pidal 2005, Menéndez Pidal-Lapesa-García 2006). It seemed reasonable to re-examine Menéndez Pidal's work critically one more time, taking into consideration these new contributions.

But there was a further reason for considering that organizing a colloquium devoted to a reappraisal of Menendez Pidal's work in Oxford was a good idea: the fact that the names of Menéndez Pidal and Oxford (more precisely, that of its University) were associated in different ways on three different occasions in the past. Ramón Menéndez Pidal visited the city of Oxford two times during his life, and apparently the name of the University of Oxford played a remarkable role in the preservation of his research materials at a particularly delicate juncture (and may have offered Menéndez Pidal a helping hand during the time he spent in exile). Associating them on a fourth opportunity seemed an appropriate way to inaugurate the series of colloquia organized by MIMSS precisely in Oxford. Perhaps the *curioso lector* will enjoy the following three snapshots of the three previous occasions on which don Ramón and Oxford saw their names appear together.

*   *   *

Chronologically, the first of these moments of contact between Menéndez Pidal and Oxford took place in June 1922, when Menéndez Pidal visited the city to receive an Honorary Degree (DLitt) from the University. Unfortunately, we do not know who suggested his candidacy for such a distinction, since the archives of the University do not record that information.[1] The honorary degree was conferred

---

[1] The procedure for the nomination of an individual for an honorary degree in the University of Oxford was as follows. An individual made a proposal for an honorary degree to Hebdomadal Council. Hebdomadal Council would then, after due consideration, accept or refuse the proposal. If accepted, the proposal was then subject to the formal approval of Convocation (at that time, the main governing body of the University). Apparently, the records of Hebdomadal Council, in accordance with the protocol of the time, maintain a high degree of confidentiality over the decision-making process behind honorary degrees, and therefore tend to be quite vague. No reasons for the proposal or the names of those who are proposed are (usually) recorded. Having checked the Hebdomadal Council minutes for 1922, this is unfortunately the case regarding Menéndez Pidal's honorary degree. The minutes for the Hebdomadal Council held on 1 May 1922 simply state that 'names were proposed for honorary degrees at the Encaenia' (Oxford University Archives, Hebdomadal Council minutes, 1/1/122, p. XIII); a vote took place on 15 May 1922 (Oxford University Archives, Hebdomadal Council minutes, 1/1/122, p. XXXII). (It might seem rather surprising to us today that the honorary degrees were still being voted on at such a late date, but apparently that was very much the usual way of doing things at this time.) A brief record of the 1922 Encaenia appeared in the

on Menéndez Pidal in the Encaenia — the annual ceremony in which the University of Oxford presents honorary degrees — which took place on 28 June 1922. Other recipients of honorary degrees at that ceremony were the former president and then Chief Justice of the United States, William H. Taft; the Lord Chancellor of England, Viscount Birkenhead; the Catholic Cardinal Francis Bourne; and the former Governor-General of South Africa, Earl Buxton. The only other honorary DLitt degree was conferred upon the poet John Masefield, soon to become (in 1930) Poet Laureate. According to the news which appeared in the local newspapers at the time, the Public Orator of the University, A. D. Godley, highlighted in his *oratio* Menéndez Pidal's contributions to the study of medieval Spanish chronicles and poetry.[2] According to the newspapers, Dr Godley said that 'there was at present in Oxford a distinct revival of interest in the language and literature of Spain, and it was especially fortunate that this should be signalised by the honour done to this eminent humanist'.[3] A few years after these words were said, in 1927, two crucial developments for the future of Spanish studies in Oxford took place: £25,000 was raised in London and given to the University to found the King Alfonso XIII Professorship of Spanish, and the Spanish Departmental Library was started.[4]

University Gazette (28 June 1922, p. 716). I wish to thank Alice Millea, Assistant Keeper of the Archives of the University, for her detailed answers to my questions.
[2]Godley's commendatory speeches on those receiving the honorary degrees were delivered in Latin (as these speeches still are today). Unfortunately Menéndez Pidal's *laudatio* was not published in Godley 1926, where some of the *orationes* delivered by Godley as Public Orator were anthologized.
[3]The quoted words appeared in *The Oxford Times*, Friday 30 June 1922, no 3189, p. 5a, and in *The Oxford Chronicle*, Friday 30 June 1922, no 4140, p. 8a. The information provided by *The Oxford Chronicle* on the 1922 Encaenia begins on p. 7a. *The Oxford Journal Illustrated* of Wednesday 5 July 1922 published on its cover a photograph of the recipients of the honorary doctorates leaving the Sheldonian Theatre, where the Encaenia ceremony took place. In that image Pidal appears in the background, to the left, standing on the threshold of the door of the Sheldonian. On page 6 there are two photographs of the procession of the participants in the ceremony from Exeter College to the Sheldonian Theatre; on the left side of one of them Pidal appears walking down Broad Street, together with the rest of the group. Two other images of Pidal in academic attire from this day (one of Pidal alone, another in the company of John Masefield and Cardinal Bourne) were published in *Estudios* (1969), between pages 272 and 273.
[4]See *100 Years of Spanish at Oxford* (2005, 'Appendix'). It might seem irrelevant, but

During this visit, his first, to Oxford, Menéndez Pidal also gave a lecture, in Spanish, in All Souls College on 26 June; its title 'Poesía popular y poesía tradicional en la literatura española'.[5] In the opening paragraphs of the lecture Menéndez Pidal says that he was invited to deliver it by W. P. Ker. At this point Ker, who had been a Fellow of All Souls since 1879, was the Professor of Poetry at the University of Oxford, a position he held until 1922; perhaps this explains the opening words of the lecture: 'El honor que me hace la invitación del Profesor Ker para dirigiros la palabra desde esta cátedra de poesía...' (Menéndez Pidal 1922: 3).[6] It is clear that Ker shared a number of research interests with Menéndez Pidal: he published on medieval epic poetry (1897) and on medieval ballads (1909); he also shared with Menéndez Pidal a strong interest in nature, mountaineering and other outdoor activities. (Indeed, Ker died of heart failure in the Pizzo Bianco, a peak in the Italian Alps, near the Swiss border, in July 1923.)[7]

It is clear that Menéndez Pidal's first contact with Oxford and its University lived up to the reputation which he had already achieved

---

it is difficult to resist the temptation to quote here the impression that, according to the local press, the Encaenia of 1922 left on some of those who were spectators to its main public part, the procession of the honorands. In an article entitled 'A Countrywoman on the Encaenia' published in *The Oxford Journal Illustrated* (5 July, 1922, 11a), we can read: 'Everyone is generally agreed that the Encaenia was a dull affair this year. A countrywoman among the many disappointed spectators was quite angry concerning the procession. "And do you mean to tell me," said she indignantly, "that that is everything? I didn't recognise a soul, and I certainly expected something more exciting. Fancy, no cheering! Though, of course, no one recognized President Taft. If I had known there was no more to be seen than that, I should have stayed at home and used my time to better advantage. Besides, there were no decent dresses to be seen".' Echoes of the *Arcipreste de Talavera* resounded in Broad Street...

[5]Published in 'Oxford, Imprenta Clarendoniana' (as it appears in the cover) that same year (Menéndez Pidal 1922). I quote from my copy, inscribed by Menéndez Pidal to Ángel González Palencia.

[6]More information on the circumstances of this invitation can be found in Catalán (2001: 268, vi–xiii). There are no documents or photographs related to Menéndez Pidal's lecture in All Souls archives. I wish to thank Norma Aubertin-Potter, Librarian-in-Charge of the Codrington Library, All Souls College, for kindly answering my questions.

[7]See Chambers (2008). An obituary for Ker, strongly focused on his passion for climbing, appears in Godley (1926, II: 87–90).

internationally as a scholar, and which had already allowed him to gather an important number of honours and distinctions.[8] The second occasion when the University of Oxford appeared in the life of Menéndez Pidal was dramatically different from the first, mostly because the circumstances also were.

When the Spanish Civil War began, Menéndez Pidal soon found himself separated from his family, when he decided to leave Spain for America after a brief sojourn in France. Apart from his own personal integrity and that of his family, there were two main concerns for Menéndez Pidal at that time: the fate of his research materials, accumulated in his home in Chamartín de la Rosa in Madrid, and the continuation of his research activity, impossible under the conditions in which Madrid, turned into a war zone, would find itself for the next three years.[9] After a short period in Bordeaux (invited by Georges Cirot) and Cuba, Menéndez Pidal needed to find permanent arrangements for an exile that turned out to be much longer than expected. He considered different options and stayed most of the time in the United States (New York) and France (Paris). It is no wonder that Menéndez Pidal received numerous invitations from different Universities in America and Europe during that period; apparently one of them came from Oxford. In what seems to be a letter, or a personal note (about which no information is provided, but which seems to have been written with Menéndez Pidal already back in Spain, where he arrived in July 1939, after his time in New York and Paris), quoted by Pérez Villanueva (1991: 371), Menéndez Pidal wrote:

---

[8]Further information about this visit to Oxford appears in Pérez Villanueva (1991: 301–302) and Pérez Pascual (1998). Pérez Villanueva says that the date of the conferral of the honorary doctorate was 26 July (instead of 28 June), and lists 'el profesor John Nesefield' as one of the honorands; he probably means John Masefield. It seems clear, given the mention of the date of the 26th, that Pérez Villanueva thought that the lecture in All Souls was part of the ceremony of the conferral of the Honorary Degree. Pérez Pascual explicitly (and wrongly) links these two events: 'En junio de 1922 Pidal recibe el doctorado honoris causa por el All Soul's [sic] College de Oxford y, en el discurso que pronunció con ese motivo, "Poesía popular y poesía tradicional en la literatura española", perfila con claridad la diferencia entre ambas expresiones' (1998: 173).

[9]This period of the life of Pidal has been masterfully and exhaustively chronicled by Diego Catalán (2001: 177–244; 2005: 109–187); see also Pérez Villanueva (1991: 341–358, 365–383) and Pérez Pascual (1998: 267–286).

> Tan necesarias eran para mí esas bibliotecas — Nueva York y
> París — que renuncié a un cómodo puesto que bondadosa-
> mente me ofrecían de parte de la Universidad de Oxford,
> como doctor 'honoris causa' que soy de ella, para que, sin
> obligación de explicar cátedra, continuara allí el interrumpido
> hilo de mis investigaciones.

Apparently, then, don Ramón was offered a research position in
Oxford. We have not found further information about this offer,[10]
although Diego Catalán seems to consider it a rather uncertain
prospect: 'Las ofertas de trabajo en Nueva York, Wisconsin, Puerto
Rico, México y Buenos Aires (que entretanto recibía) eran, ante la
prolongación de la Guerra Civil, más dignas de atención que las
dudosas posibilidades de que las universidades de Oxford o Burdeos
pudieran acogerle durante un tiempo largo' (2005: 115n14; see also
Catalán 2001: 186).

However this was not the only contact between Menéndez Pidal
and the University of Oxford during the years of the Spanish Civil
War: there was another one, interestingly enough unsuspected by
Menéndez Pidal — and probably by the University of Oxford as well
—, and perhaps crucial for the preservation of his library and part of
his research materials. During the three years he was forced to spend
outside Spain, Menéndez Pidal was very worried about the fate of his
research materials (especially those he gathered over the years for the
elaboration of his *Historia de la lengua española*, and those related to the
Romancero) and of his library. Diego Catalán, in the study he wrote
as a companion volume to the posthumous edition of Menéndez
Pidal's *Historia de la lengua española* (Catalán 2005), describes in detail
the remarkable movements of those materials, unscathed by war and
by the different changes of location they experienced. There, and in
other writings on Menéndez Pidal's life and work, Catalán explains
that his house in La Cuesta del Zarzal, 23, Chamartín, and the library

---

[10]I have examined the Minutes of the meetings of the Board of the Faculty of Medieval
and Modern Languages and Literatures of the University of Oxford and the reports
sent to the said Board for the period 1936–39, and no mention whatsoever of
a possible invitation to Menéndez Pidal to take a research position in Oxford
was found. If such an invitation was made, albeit informally, perhaps Professor
Entwistle, then King Alfonso XIII Professor of Spanish, and always on good terms
with Menéndez Pidal with whom he shared research interests (Spanish ballads and
History of the Spanish Language), was the one who made it.

and archives housed in it, also survived the war unscathed — despite all the violence and vandalism that took place in Madrid during the period 1936–1939. It is interesting to see what seems to be one of the reasons for the house remaining untouched.

In a letter to Menéndez Pidal (who was still in Paris) written on 22 April 1939 from Madrid —just three weeks after the end of the war —, María Goyri wrote:

> La conservación de la casa se debe principalmente al vecino [=*Juan López Suárez*], que la ha defendido con mil artimañas, por eso me indigna que el energúmeno del sobrinito [=*Luis Menéndez Pidal*] le haya vejado cuanto ha podido a causa de su parentesco con Pepe Claudio [=*José Castillejo*]. También a la infeliz Maximina [*la guardesa de Cuesta del Zarzal 23 cuyo único hijo había muerto luchando del lado republicano*] le dio un par de coces, diciéndole que ahora tenía él mucho más duro el corazón. Figúrate cómo estará.[11]

Juan López Suárez appears here as 'vecino' of the Menéndez Pidal family and as a relative — more precisely, brother-in-law, since he married his sister, Mariana — of José Castillejo, the professor of Law, Krausist intellectual and pedagogue founder of the *Instituto-Escuela*, and Secretary of the Junta de Ampliación de Estudios. This fits, since we know that Menéndez Pidal's house in Chamartín is built in the so-called 'Olivar de Castillejo' (known previously as 'Olivar del Balcón'), an area full of olive trees bought in 1917 by Castillejo where he built his own house and then sold the rest of the land to other professors and intellectuals related to the Junta de Ampliación de Estudios, such as Ignacio Bolívar, Luis Lozano Rey and Ramón Menéndez Pidal, who also decided to build his house there in 1925.[12]

---

[11]I quote from Catalán (2001: 246), maintaining the clarifications he made between brackets. The elusiveness of the allusions to other people and the use of aliases (such as 'Pepe Claudio') were due to the censorship to which all personal correspondence was subject during these years. Indeed, many of the letters of the war period written by Menéndez Pidal or members of his family which Catalán quotes (2001, 2005) frequently use aliases or some sort of ciphered language. This fragment is also quoted in Pérez Pascual (1998: 286). See also Catalán (2005: 182). Luis Menéndez Pidal, Ramón's nephew (son of his brother Luis, a famous painter), was an architect, and he had designed and built Pidal's house in Chamartín.

[12]See Catalán 2001: 112n223 and Catalán & Castillejo 2005. The preservation of this

During the Spanish Civil War both José Castillejo and Menéndez Pidal (and their families) were away from their homes in the Olivar,[13] and Juan López Suárez (together, presumably, with his wife) was the only one of the usual residents who stayed there (Catalán & Castillejo 2005: 'Etapa de 1936–1945'; Fandiño 2003: 17, 144). He, together with the *guardeses* (the abovementioned Maximina and her husband, Juan Jaro) played a crucial role in maintaining the integrity of the houses during three years of war and destruction. We can find out more about the 'mil artimañas' used by Juan López Suárez in a letter written by Jimena, Menéndez Pidal's daughter, to her father on 22 June 1939:

> Vengo del Zarzal, donde todo está intacto gracias a la defensa heroica de Maximina y López Suárez, el que hizo que un huésped suyo inglés (sobrino de Ba[i]ll[y]-Ba[i]ll[i]ère) pusiese el sello de protección inglesa por tener en la biblioteca libros de la Universidad de Oxford, cosa absurda que valió (Catalán 2001: 246n5).[14]

olivar (as a natural and cultural heritage of the utmost importance) from the greed of estate developers and businessmen, and from the stupidity of local politicians, was the struggle to which Diego Catalán devoted most of his time and energies in the last years of his life until his death on 9 April 2008. Written testimony of that struggle can be seen in the multiple sections of the webpage *En defensa del Olivar de Chamartín* <http://olivarchamartin.blogia.com/>. About Juan López Suárez's life, see Fandiño (2003). Surprisingly enough, Fandiño (and some of his sources) say that it was not Castillejo who bought the Olivar, but López Suárez, who later sold parts of it to Castillejo, Bolívar, Menéndez Pidal, etc. (Fandiño 2003: 18, 117). To all the references already quoted about this particular, see what María Goyri wrote in a letter (full of complaints about the builder's work in the construction of Pidal's house in Chamartín) sent to Jimena Menéndez Pidal and Miguel Catalán on 23 November 1924: 'El terreno que era de Camuño, es decir lo que queda del olivar después de lo de Castillejo, lo ha comprado López Suárez para hacerse una casa' (Castillejo 1999: 560).

[13]The reason for Castillejo's absence are given in Pérez Pascual (1998: 269).

[14]Quoted also by Pérez Pascual (1998: 285). I have been unable to find any reference to which member of the Bailly-Baillière family this allusion may refer to. The Bailly-Baillière family had a publishing house and a library in the Plaza de Santa Ana in Madrid, where they published not only books of medicine and sciences — the traditional trade of the family in France —, but also such an influential series as the *Nueva Biblioteca de Autores Españoles* — where Pidal published his first edition of the *Primera Crónica General*. Jean-Baptiste Baillière, the patriarch of this family of publishers, sent his nephew, Charles François Bailly (1825–1909), to Madrid, as part of his expansion plans: 'In 1848, in Madrid, Jean-Baptiste's nephew Charles

More details about this remarkable development are provided in
Catalán & Castillejo (2005: 'Etapa de 1936–1945'):

> El arquitecto Sánchez Arcas […], con mando en las brigadas
> de Trabajo Social de las Milicias Populares del Quinto Regi-
> miento, propuso a Menéndez Pidal llevar su biblioteca a lugar
> seguro, ante el posible avance hacia Chamartín de *los moros*,
> que ocupaban ya la Casa de Campo; pero Menéndez Pidal,
> que iba a embarcarse con destino a la Universidad de Burdeos,
> prefirió dejar pasar la casa como cosa sin valor y no vaciarla.
> Juan López Suárez consiguió entonces que todo el Olivar
> quedara bajo la protección de la bandera inglesa, y alquiló la
> casa de su cuñado [=*i.e., José Castillejo*] (refugiado en Londres)
> a J. Walters, el propietario del periódico londinense *The Times*.
> López Suárez hizo un boquete en el muro de separación con
> la casa de Menéndez Pidal para tener fácil acceso a ella y
> selló su biblioteca con escritos de protección a nombre de la
> Universidad de Oxford. Cuando Arturo Ruiz Castillo, Pedro
> González Quijano y otros milicianos pretendieron trasladar
> la biblioteca de Menéndez Pidal, consiguió mantenerla en su
> sitio.[15]

François Bailly (1825–1909), known as Carlos Bailly-Baillière, translated and edited
French authors for the Spanish-speaking medical students. Carlos even founded a
printing works. The Bailly-Baillière books were exported to the Spanish colonies
of South America. His sons Antonio (1866–1909) and Enrique Bailly (1864–?)
took over the bookshop, which finally disappeared in the torments of the Spanish
civil war in 1936' (Regnier 2005: 93). Was this Enrique Bailly the uncle of the
mysterious Englishman who lived in Castillejo's house? See note 18 below for
further hypotheses.

[15]Apparently this was not the only *artimaña* used by López Suárez to protect
Menéndez Pidal's library: 'É moi coñecido o episodio que narra como López Suárez
lle salvou a biblioteca a D. Ramón Menéndez Pidal en plena guerra civil. Don
Juan residía en Madrid, na súa casa do Zarzal dos Pinares de Chamartín [*sic*].
Un día presentáronse uns milicianos na casa de D. Ramón e os criados avisaron
de forma inmediata a López Suárez que acudiu con toda rapidez e con ánimo de
impresionalos e de asustalos. Díxolles en ton desafiante que aquela era a biblioteca
de Menéndez Pidal. Os milicianos confundiron ao eminente filólogo con Menéndez
Pelayo e retiráronse respetuosamente farfallando polo baixo: "¡Ah! Esta es la
famosa biblioteca de Menéndez Pelayo".' (Fandiño 2003: 19). In all likelihood, had
the *milicianos* been more familiar with don Marcelino's ideas and principles, López
Suárez's initiative could have seriously backfired. About the help López Suárez
received from Gonzalo Menéndez Pidal (don Ramón's son) to hide a number of
pieces of jewellery in the basement of his house, see the text by Moure Mariño
quoted by Fandiño (2003: 126).

Who was really the person renting Castillejo's house? The information 'J. Walters, el propietario del periódico londinense *The Times*' seems to be accurate, since John Walter (1873–1968; not Walters) was by 1936–39 the co-proprietor of *The Times*.[16] He was the great-great-grandson of John Walter, who founded *The Times* in 1785, and some aspects of his biography seem extremely relevant for our purposes today: 'He was based in Madrid as *The Times*'s correspondent for the Iberian peninsula at the time his father died [1910]. He had a lifelong affection for Spain. He spent the years 1916–18 as publicity attaché at the British embassy in Madrid, countering German propaganda; his elder son, John, was to serve in the embassy's press section in the Second World War' (Haley 2004). Considering Walter was already 63 when the Civil War started (a quite advanced age on those years), and given the fact that his son seemed also to have connections with Madrid in the following years, the chances are that the 'huésped suyo [= de Castillejo] inglés' could have been his son. (No information about John Walter *iunior* appears in the *Oxford Dictionary of National Biography*).[17] However, the most likely scenario is to consider that the person staying in Castillejo's house was Ernest de Caux, who was

---

[16]In 1922, on the death of Alfred Harmsworth, 1st Viscount Northcliffe, owner of *The Times*, 'his will decreed that John Walter, whose family had owned *The Times* from its foundation until 1908, should have the first option to buy, but Walter did not possess the £1.5 million necessary to do so. Northcliffe's brother Lord Rothermere now seemed all set to take over the 'Thunderer' [i.e., *The Times*]. Then, enter Major Astor. He was determined not to see *The Times* fall back under Harmsworth control and wanted, as he said, 'to secure as far as possible the continued independence of one great journal, and through it the perpetuation of the highest standards of British journalism' […]. In December 1922 he acquired a 90 per cent shareholding and became co-proprietor with Walter.' (Wilson 2008). Astor was Chief Proprietor of the paper until 1966 (see 'Astor of Hever' 2007). Walter seemed to be quite happy with his secondary role at the helm of the newspaper, obtained thanks to Astor money: 'He stayed much the junior partner in a stable relationship, and his chief proprietorship, involving by that time only responsibility for the appointment and dismissal of the editor, lasted until The Times and the Sunday Times were merged under Lord Thomson of Fleet on 1 January 1967, when his family's long connection with The Times came to an end' (Haley 2004).

[17]In any case, it might be interesting to point out that John Walter, the co-proprietor of *The Times*, had studied in Oxford, at Christ Church — where he obtained a rather disappointing Third in *Litterae Humaniores* in 1897 (Haley 2004) —, and therefore could have had access to any Oxford-related stationery which he could have shared with Juan López Suárez in an attempt to protect Menéndez Pidal's library.

for many years the correspondent of *The Times* in Madrid, and who in fact lived for many years there and died in the same city in 1960 (see his obituary in *The Times*, Tuesday 29 March 1960, p. 17*a*). It is tempting to see in his French surname and in his French links (he was a student in Paris and Rennes) a hint that could identify him with the 'sobrino de Ba[i]ll[y]-Ba[i]ll[i]ère' mentioned in Jimena Menéndez-Pidal's letter quoted above, but I could not find any information to that effect.[18]

That the episode is true seems to be guaranteed by the reliability of the sources quoted — María Goyri, Jimena Menéndez Pidal and Diego Catalán (wife, daughter and grandson of Menéndez Pidal) —; but we also have direct testimony from Menéndez Pidal himself about this episode. Unfortunately, it appears in a rather unreliable source. In 1946 Warren F. Manning, a North American professor of Medieval French Literature at West Virginia University, paid a visit to Menéndez Pidal in his house in Chamartín. He published shortly thereafter a brief memoir of his conversation with Menéndez Pidal in *Hispania* (Manning 1946). In a passage of that text, Manning wrote:

> On returning to Madrid, he has found that his home had been stripped by the Loyalists (*bandidos* was the term he used in referring to them) of all its belongings, his books, papers, card-index files, paintings and other works of art. However, a quick-witted neighbor had posted a sign upon his door which read as follows: 'This house is the property of Señor Menéndez Pidal, doctor *honoris causa* of the University of Oxford ('Which was true', said Menéndez Pidal), and is under the special protection of the British Embassy ('Which was not true', he added.' As a consequence, although the intruders did not refrain from stripping the house, they did not dare destroy their loot; and all of the property was recovered in Geneva, where it lay carefully boxed up and in perfect order. 'Even

---

[18]Fandiño (2003: 18) mentions that 'Ernest de Caux, correpondente de The Times de Londres' was the person who gave shelter in his house in Madrid to José Castillejo before he could leave Madrid for Alicante, from where he flew to London. De Caux is presented as an exceptionally well informed correspondent both in the abovementioned obituary and in Thomas (1994: 156). Fact and legend could start being commingled if we consider the identity of one of the correspondents sent by *The Times* to cover the Spanish Civil War: none other than Kim Philby (Clive 2004). Did he stay during his time in Madrid in Menéndez Pidal's house, turned into some sort of delegation of *The Times* in Madrid?

my card-index files were undisturbed,' said Menéndez Pidal.
'Come and see for yourself.' And he led me into his library,
where he pulled out drawer after drawer of index cards (521).

Of course, what Manning says here about Menéndez Pidal's house
being looted is absolutely false;[19] but it is interesting to see that don
Ramón mentioned the subterfuge that served, apparently, to protect
his house and his research materials from any potential danger. Be
it as it may, the name of the University of Oxford seems to have
been associated with Menéndez Pidal during the adverse times of
the Spanish Civil War both in the form of an invitation to occupy
a research position in it and also as part of a rather farfetched,
but still apparently effective, strategy to preserve Menéndez Pidal's
house, library and research materials during the years of the Spanish
Civil War (even if that intervention was in all likelihood completely
unknown to anyone in Oxford, and ultimately a blatant lie).

The third Oxonian connection in Menéndez Pidal's life is marked
by his second visit to Oxford, in 1962, in order to participate in the
first meeting of the Asociación Internacional de Hispanistas. He
was elected first 'Presidente de honor' of the AIH, and presented
a rather controversial paper — especially for a 93 year-old scholar
— on Father Las Casas. In the opening words of his plenary paper
Menéndez Pidal reminisced about the days of his previous visit to
Oxford:

Ante todo me permitiréis una digresión de mi tema, para
mostrar mi grata emoción al verme en esta ciudad, al vestir
de nuevo su toga universitaria, y al recordar la encaenia [sic]
de 1922 en que recibí el doctorado honoris causa; deseo rendir

---

[19]As a matter of fact, Menéndez Pidal sent a correction to the editor of the journal
where Manning published his note, denying any wrongdoing to his property: 'No
pude decir que mi casa de Madrid había sido saqueada por bandidos ningunos, pues
la encontré en perfecto estado de conservación a pesar de los tres años de guerra
y abandono; no dejé en ella más que a los porteros, y ni las ramas de los árboles
habían sido cortadas, a pesar de los fríos inviernos. Mis papeles de trabajo no fueron
sacados de mi casa, sino de un edificio extranjero donde yo los había depositado
y aparecieron efectivamente en Ginebra, cuidadosamente embalados' (Menéndez
Pidal 1947: 226; see also Pérez Pascual 1998: 285). Pidal's correction is followed
by a rather reluctant note by Manning, which proves right the view of this person
provided by Catalán (2001: 244). Concerning the preservation of Pidal's research
materials, see Catalán (2001, 2005).

un tributo a la memoria del profesor W. P. Ker, cuya amistad entonces gané. Él, con sus trabajos sobre la épica germánica, me ilustró, él me invitó a que hiciese aquí una primera exposición global de mis ideas sobre la poesía popular (Menéndez Pidal 1964: 13)

Frank Pierce, in his chronicle of the first 25 years of the AIH, attested to Menéndez Pidal's support for the newly created association, rather than the counter-initiative sponsored by the government of Madrid (Pierce 1986: 3–4). Menéndez Pidal's biographers have chronicled this episode,[20] as have some of those who were in Oxford participating in the conference. Alan Deyermond, for instance, has rightly highlighted a particularly intense moment:

El día había comenzado con la ponencia inaugural sobre Las Casas que pronunció Ramón Menéndez Pidal, vestido con la toga de un doctor de Oxford. Nos recordó que ya había estado allí cuarenta años antes, en 1922, para recibir un doctorado honoris causa (desde 1920 era académico correspondiente de la British Academy). La ponencia de don Ramón ('Don Pidal', según el Rector de la Universidad de Oxford) provocó un debate tan animado con Marcel Bataillon que el ponente avanzó gesticulando varias veces hasta el borde de la plataforma, haciéndonos temer que muriera a los 93 años cayendo como Calisto (aunque por razones muy distintas). Se divertía tanto en el congreso (en el que fue nombrado Presidente de Honor de la recién nacida AIH) que alguien me comentó: 'Don Ramón es el más joven de todos los congresistas'. [...] Lo que más siento de aquel congreso es que no me atreví a saludarle (era muy consciente de que acababa de regresar de hacer mis investigaciones en Palencia, y de que ellas darían lugar a un libro nada neotradicionalista sobre las Mocedades de Rodrigo) (Deyermond 2001: 18).[21]

Very recently some anecdotal, yet interesting, aspects of the *intrahistoria* of this last visit by Menéndez Pidal to Oxford were chronicled precisely by the person who in many ways indelibly shaped Hispanic

---

[20]Pérez Villanueva (1991: 492–493), Pérez Pascual (1998: 363). The latter wrongly dates this last visit to Oxford to 1963.

[21]This episode is reflected in Pérez Pascual's biography (1998: 363), taken from the account offered in Gaos (1968).

studies in Oxford in the 20th century: Sir Peter Russell. I cannot help quoting here the lines in which Russell — in an otherwise not so pro-Pidalian article — describes Menéndez Pidal's arrival in Heathrow, and Russell's attempts to bring up at some point during the car trip to Oxford his 1952 article on the *Poema de Mio Cid*:

> In 1962 on the occasion of the first meeting here of the Aso-ciación Internacional de Hispanistas I was deputed to go to Heathrow to bring him to Oxford in my car — a job I willingly took on because I thought that, as I had been told he would be travelling alone, he would be bound to make an allusion to my work on the Cid during the drive. Nothing went according to plan. I had got permission to park at the very entrance to the terminal after explaining to the police that I was there to pick up a distinguished but very frail Spanish scholar of ninety-three who would probably be in a wheelchair. This ploy was rather discredited when don Ramón emerged walking at a spanking pace past the policeman concerned. He was unexpectedly followed slowly by his groaning ex-pupil Dámaso Alonso who, though a frequent air traveller, always claimed plane travel brought him to the verge of extinction. Don Ramón immediately asked me if we could make a detour on the way to Oxford so that he could see Windsor Castle again. That we duly did, but with don Dámaso orally wilting in the back seat there was no opportunity to ask the master if he knew of my article of ten years before. He certainly made no mention of it then, or ever (Russell 2002: 68).

It is truly amazing to see in these two first-hand accounts of Menén-dez Pidal's visit to Oxford in 1962 the liveliness and the dynamism of that 93 year-old professor who seemed to be enjoying his presence in that meeting as a doctoral candidate would enjoy his or her first participation in a conference.[22]

---

[22]Nevertheless, those Oxonian days were tainted by the sadness produced by the absence in Oxford of a scholar who Menéndez Pidal was very much looking forward to meeting there, María Rosa Lida de Malkiel: 'Cuando fui al Congreso Internacional de Hispanistas, que se celebraba en Oxford por setiembre del pasado año 1962, uno de los alicientes que allá llevaba era el conocer a doña María Rosa, la escritora que yo tanto admiraba y que allí iba a presentar una memoria sobre la ''Función del cuento popular en el *Lazarillo*''. Pero mi deseo se vio tristemente

These are the three moments in which the life of Ramón Menéndez Pidal and the city of Oxford and its University met. In a different manner, the colloquium in which a group of distinguished scholars reassessed the continuing vitality of the work of Menéndez Pidal forty years after his death, and this volume of proceedings which reflects the written versions of the papers presented there, wished to extend this connection between don Ramón and the city of the dreaming spires.

*   *   *

This volume, and the conference from which it originated, has a debt of gratitude with a number of persons and institutions. In the first place, to the President and Fellows of Magdalen College, who supported the proposal for the creation of MIMSS, and who keep the seminar going with their support. In the second place, to all the participants in the seminar, who kindly accepted my invitation to participate in this colloquium about Menéndez Pidal's work. They all presented excellent papers, and they have sent them for publication in this volume, respecting deadlines and editorial norms, something for which, as the editor of the volume, I feel enormously grateful. I also wish to thank Alan Deyermond for opening the doors of the Papers of the Medieval Hispanic Research Seminar to this volume and, hopefully, for more MIMSS-born volumes in the future. My gratitude also goes to all those, colleagues (from Oxford or from elsewhere) and students (ditto), who attended the sessions of the colloquium. A special mention has to be made of the names of Alan Deyermond, David G. Pattison and Geraldine Coates: in their role as members of the advisory board of MIMSS they provided essential advice and guidance for the planning and the organization of the colloquium.

---

frustrado al noticiarme el Profesor Malkiel que su esposa no había podido asistir al Congreso a causa del agravamiento de la enfermedad que padecía. Apenas regresé a Madrid, escribí a la enferma diciéndole cuánto era mi sentimiento por no haberla encontrado en Oxford, y animándola cuanto era posible respecto a su salud. Su contestación, Berkeley, 18 de setiembre de 1962, fue desoladora, despidiéndose de mí con frases de conmovedor afecto y despidiéndose de la vida con la más serena conformidad' (Menéndez Pidal 1963: 7).

But my biggest debt of gratitude is tainted with sadness. When putting together the colloquium, it was obvious for me that one of the participants had to be Diego Catalán. As everybody knows, he has been not only the one who has done more over the years for the preservation of the Pidalian intellectual heritage, but also the one who first, and in many cases most strongly, criticized Menéndez Pidal's ideas — his research into the *Estoria de España*, for instance, provided a substantial revision of the map of Alfonsine and post-Alfonsine historiography drafted by don Ramón. When in July 2007 I contacted Diego Catalán and asked him to participate in the MIMSS colloquium on Menéndez Pidal, he was embarked on his struggle for the preservation of the Pidalian heritage from the miserable attempts by some devious businessmen and conniving politicians to turn what Diego has rightly labelled a *patrimonio de la Humanidad* into an outrageously profitable real estate operation, with a complete disregard for the uniqueness of Menéndez Pidal's house and the research materials stored in it. He chronicled many of the chapters of his struggle in http://olivarchamartin.blogia.com/, and was able to get the support of many researchers and institutions (as can be seen in http://olivarchamartin.blogia.com/temas/cartas-de-los-amigos-del-olivar-de-chamartin.php).

In spite of all this, Diego found time to reply kindly to my request. Here is the text of the e-mail I received from him on 12 September 2007:

> Tu plan para 2008 me parece una contribución magnífica a la 'celebración' del 40º aniversario de la muerte de RMP (en la acepción 3ª, más que en la 4ª del verbo 'celebrar', ya que no es pertinente 'alegrarse' de su muerte, por más tiempo que haya pasado desde ella). Lo creo muy apropiado, además de por su interés en sí (dados los participantes), como apoyo al proyecto en que estoy comprometido: el intentar, en ese año, conseguir, gracias al apoyo internacional, la tramitación de la declaración de los Archivos depositados en la 'Casa Menéndez Pidal' (junto con la 'Casa' y el 'Olivar de Chamartín') parte del Patrimonio Universal. Si no lo consigo ese año, todo acabará destruyéndose, perdiéndose para las generaciones futuras. Es tarea dura y complicada, dado el panorama nacional y el concepto oficial de lo que constituye la 'Cultura' en España; pero la respuesta (vuestra respuesta) de la gente pensante ha

sido tan espléndida, que es el momento adecuado para dar la batalla. Mi apoyo y contribución a tus planes, más que con mi presencia en Oxford, creo que podría articularse mediante una carta-escrito dirigida por mí 'A la Universidad de Oxford en el 40º aniversario de la muerte de Ramón Menéndez Pidal', en que cabría sumariar pasado y futuro...¿Qué te parece?

Diego Catalán

My answer, of course, was that I was extremely happy with his suggestion, and that I was looking forward to receiving his text, which would be read in the colloquium and printed in its proceedings. By February 2008 I started to think that perhaps it was time to send Diego a friendly reminder. So I did, but no answer arrived. Which was not surprising at all, since Diego was not particularly quick in replying, and, in general, not so keen on using e-mail. On the other hand, the blog posts about his last book project — an edition and study of the so-called *Cancionero en cifra de Perrenot*[23] — were a clear sign of Diego being busy with his research projects, and (I inferred, and wrongly so) perhaps then the text he would send to Oxford would be next in the pipeline. By the end of March I was beginning to be slightly worried (only slightly: Diego was particularly good at meeting deadlines just by the skin of his teeth), and on 12 April 2008, while I was browsing through the newspaper, killing time in Barajas while waiting for the plane which would bring me back home after a visit to Salamanca, I was thinking that I must call Diego once I was back home to see when the text would arrive. At that precise moment I saw in *El País* the *esquela* with the news of Diego's death, on 9 April.

There is something missing in this volume, then; something that leaves a gap nothing can fill. But it was impossible for Diego Catalán's name to be absent from the pages of this volume: his name appears in all the contributions. Thus, in the same way that — in a very Cidian fashion — his fight for Menéndez Pidal's heritage turned into a victory achieved after his death (on 26 February 2009 the Government of Madrid declared the Olivar de Chamartín protected

---

[23]They can be found in http://olivarchamartin.blogia.com/, under the titles 'Prólogo al *Cancionero en cifra de Perrenot*' and 'Índice del libro *La enigmática carta del embajador, 28 de mayo / 6 de junio de 1562*'.

by law), his words and his ideas appear in these pages. In addition, in the same way that we decided to dedicate the colloquium we held in May 2008 to his memory, we wish now to dedicate this volume to his memory as well.

Oxford, March 2009[24]

Postscript. The sad news of the death of Alan Deyermond hit when the manuscript of this book was receiving the final touches before being sent to the printers. His contribution to this volume will perhaps have the dubious honour of being his first posthumous publication. For many reasons, we wish to dedicate this volume also to the memory of Alan Deyermond.

Oxford, September 2009

---

[24] I wish to express here my gratitude to Roger Wright for revising this article. His help has been fundamental for turning my rather infelicitous prose into proper English.

Works Cited

100 Years of Spanish at Oxford, 2005. 100 Years of Spanish at Oxford [http://www.mod-langs.ox.ac.uk/spanish/100years/, accessed 18 March 2009].

'Astor of Hever', 2007. 'Astor of Hever, 1st Baron'. In *Who Was Who, A & C Black, 1920–2008*; online edn, Oxford University Press, Dec 2007 [*sic!*] [http://www.ukwhoswho.com/view/article/oupww/whowaswho/ U151864, accessed 20 March 2009].

CASTILLEJO, David, 1999. *Epistolario de José Castillejo. III. Fatalidad y porvenir (1913–1937)*. Madrid: Castalia.

CATALÁN, Diego, 1992. 'Presentación de la obra', in Ramón Menéndez Pidal, *La épica medieval española. Desde sus orígenes hasta su disolución en el Romancero*. Ed. Diego Catalán & María del Mar Bustos. Obras completas de R. Menéndez Pidal, XIII. Madrid: Espasa Calpe.

——, 2001. *El Archivo del Romancero, patrimonio de la Humanidad. Historia documentada de un siglo de historia*. Madrid: Fundación Ramón Menéndez Pidal & Seminario Menéndez Pidal.

——, 2005. '"Una catedral para una lengua". (Introducción a la *Historia de la Lengua de Menéndez Pidal*)', in Ramón Menéndez Pidal, *Historia de la Lengua Española*. Ed. Diego Catalán (Madrid: FRMP & RAE), II, 77–265.

CATALÁN, Diego & David CASTILLEJO, 2005. 'Historia del Olivar', in *Amigos de El Olivar* [http://www.elolivardechamartin.com/hist/historia1.php; also in http://olivarchamartin.blogia.com/2005/052501-historia-del-olivar-de-chamartin-i.php, accessed 20 March 2009].

CHAMBERS, R. W, 2008. 'Ker, William Paton (1855–1923)', rev. A. S. G. Edwards, *Oxford Dictionary of National Biography*, Oxford: Oxford UP, 2004; online edition, Oct 2008 [http://www.oxforddnb.com/view/article/34298, accessed 17 March 2009].

CLIVE, Nigel, 2004. 'Philby, Harold Adrian Russell [Kim] (1912–1988)', rev., *Oxford Dictionary of National Biography*, Oxford: Oxford UP. [http://www.oxforddnb.com/view/article/40699, accessed 20 March 2009.]

CONDE, Juan-Carlos, 2007. 'Welcome to MIMSS', in *MIMSS. Magdalen Iberian Medieval Studies Seminar* [http://mimss-english.blogspot.com/, accessed 24 March 2009].

DEYERMOND, Alan, ed. 1992–93. 'Ramón Menéndez Pidal twenty-five years on', *Journal of Hispanic Research*, 2: 125–142.

——, 2001. 'Mansa pobreza', *Boletín de la Asociación Internacional de Hispanistas*, 8: 17–18.

Estudios, 1969. 'Estudios sobre la personalidad y la obra de Menéndez Pidal' and 'Estudios en memoria de Menéndez Pidal', *Cuadernos Hispanoamericanos*, 238–240 (Octubre-Diciembre).

FANDIÑO, Xosé Ramón, 2003. *Juan López Suárez ou 'Xan de Forcados'*. Sada: Ediciós do Castro.

GAOS, Vicente, 1968. 'Grandioso don Ramón', *Índice*, 238: 33–35.

GODLEY, A. D., 1926. *Reliquiae*. Ed. C.R.L. Fletcher. Oxford: Oxford UP, 2 vols.

HALEY, William, 2004. 'Walter, John (1873–1968)', *Oxford Dictionary of National Biography*, Oxford: Oxford UP; online ed. [http://www.oxforddnb.com/view/article/36718, accessed 20 March 2009].

HEMPEL, Wido & Dietrich BRIESEMEISTER , eds., 1982. *Actas del Coloquio hispano-alemán Ramón Menéndez Pidal (Madrid, 31 de marzo a 2 de abril de 1978)*. Tübingen: Max Niemeyer Verlag.

KER, W. P, 1897. *Epic and romance. Essays on medieval literature*. London: Macmillan.

——, 1909. 'On the history of the ballads (1100–1500)', *Proceedings of the British Academy*, 4: 179–205.

MANNING, Warren F., 1946. 'A Visit to Menéndez Pidal', *Hispania*, 29.4: 519–522.

MENÉNDEZ PIDAL, Ramón, 1896. *La leyenda de los Infantes de Lara*. Madrid: Imprenta de Ducazcal.

——, 1922. *Poesía popular y poesía tradicional en la literatura española. Conferencia leída en All Souls College, el lunes día 26 de Junio de 1922, por Ramón Menéndez Pidal*. Oxford: Imprenta Clarendoniana.

——, 1947. 'Correction', *Hispania*, 30.2: 226.

——, 1963. 'Prólogo', *RPh*, 17: 5–8.

——, 1964. 'Observaciones críticas sobre las biografías de Fray Bartolomé de las Casas', in *Actas del Primer Congreso Internacional de Hispanistas, celebrado en Oxford del 6 al 11 de septiembre de 1962*. Ed. Frank Pierce & Cyril A. Jones. Oxford: The Dolphin Book Co. Ltd. for the Asociación Internacional de Hispanistas, pp. 13–24.

——, 1992. *La épica medieval española. Desde sus orígenes hasta su disolución en el Romancero*. Ed. Diego Catalán & María del Mar Bustos. Obras completas de R. Menéndez Pidal, XIII. Madrid: Espasa Calpe.

——, 2005. *Historia de la lengua española*. Ed. Diego Catalán. Madrid: FRMP & RAE.

——, Rafael LAPESA & Constantino GARCÍA , 2003. *Léxico hispánico primitivo (siglos VIII al XII). Versión primera del 'Glosario del primitivo léxico iberorrománico'*. Ed. Manuel Seco. Madrid: FRMP & RAE.

PÉREZ PASCUAL, José Ignacio, 1998. *Ramón Menéndez Pidal: ciencia y pasión*. Valladolid: Consejería de Educación y Cultura, Junta de Castilla y León.

PÉREZ VILLANUEVA, Joaquín, 1991. *Ramón Menéndez Pidal: su vida y su tiempo*. Madrid: Espasa-Calpe.

PIERCE, Frank, 1986. *Asociación Internacional de Hispanistas. Fundación e Historia 1962–1986. En homenaje al IX Congreso de la Asociación Internacional de Hispanistas en el Instituto Iberoamericano del Patrimonio Cultural Prusiano*.

Berlín, 18–23 de agosto de 1986. [Sheffield: the author, 1986]. Also available online [http://asociacioninternacionaldehispanistas.org/pierce.html]

RÉGNIER, Christian, 2005. 'Jean-Baptiste Baillière (1797–1885). The pioneering publisher who promoted French medicine throughout the world', *Medicographia*, 27.1: 87–96 [http://www.medicographia.com/html/static/html/issues/82/art_13/article.pdf, accessed 20 March 2009].

RUSSELL, Peter E., 2002. 'Reinventing an Epic Poet: 1952 in Context', in *'Mio Cid' Studies: 'Some problems of Diplomatic' Fifty Years On*. Ed. Alan Deyermond, David G. Pattison & Eric Southworth. PMHRS, 42. London: Department of Hispanic Studies, Queen Mary, University of London, pp. 63–71.

THOMAS, Hugh, 1994. *The Spanish Civil War*. New York: Touchstone.

WILSON, Derek, 2008. 'Astor, John Jacob, first Baron Astor of Hever (1886–1971)', *Oxford Dictionary of National Biography*, Oxford: Oxford UP, 2004; online ed., revised Jan 2008 [http://www.oxforddnb.com/view/article/30773, accessed 20 March 2009]

Menéndez Pidal and the Epic

ALAN DEYERMOND

(Queen Mary)

1. Introduction

Six years ago, a few hundred yards away from this room, a group of hispanomedievalists (some present today) met to discuss and commemorate Peter Russell's brilliantly iconoclastic article, 'Some Problems of Diplomatic in the *Cantar de Mio Cid* and their Implications' (1952); the papers and discussions were published a few months later (*Cid* 2002). It is appropriate to begin today's survey of Menéndez Pidal's work and its present standing with a discussion of his work on the epic: appropriate both because of this local relevance and because the epic is where Menéndez Pidal's research began.

The local relevance goes further than the 2002 Oxford symposium. Let me quote, with one correction, what I wrote fifteen years ago (1992–93: 136):

> In view of what used to be widely believed in Spain and elsewhere, and of what is occasionally said even now, it is worth recording that British admiration for Menéndez Pidal has a long history. He was elected a Corresponding Fellow of the British Academy in 1920 (his only Spanish predecessor, Marcelino Menéndez y Pelayo, elected in 1909, had died in 1912). The University of Oxford conferred an honorary degree in 1922, and his lecture on that occasion, delivered at All Souls College, was published by the [Clarendon] Press (Menéndez Pidal 1922). In 1962, at the age of 93, he was invited back to Oxford for the first congress of the Asociación Internacional de Hispanistas, organized by the AHGBI, and was elected Presidente de Honor. His plenary paper at the congress shows (1964: 13) that the admiration that British scholars felt for him was reciprocated: 'Ante todo me permitiréis una digresión de mi tema, para mostrar mi grata emoción al verme en esta ciudad, al vestir de nuevo su toga universitaria, y al recordar la encaenia de 1922 en que recebí el doctorado *honoris causa*; deseo rendir un tributo a la memoria del profesor W. P. Ker cuya amistad entonces gané. Él, con sus trabajos sobre la

épica germánica, me ilustró; él me invitó a que hiciese aquí una primera exposición global de mis ideas sobre la poesía popular [1922].'

In 1892 the Real Academia Española held a prize competition for a 'Gramática y vocabulario del *Poema del Cid*', and the twenty-three-year-old Ramón Francisco Antonio Leandro Menéndez Pidal was one of the entrants (his little-known full name is one of many nuggets of information supplied by José Ignacio Pérez Pascual's excellent biography published in 1998).[1] Four years later he published his first book, *La leyenda de los Infantes de Lara* (1896). Not long before his death in late 1968 he was still hoping to publish his long-planned *Historia de la épica*, of which a good deal existed in draft (thanks to the selfless labours of Diego Catalán and María del Mar Bustos, his drafts have been edited to form a coherent volume on *La épica medieval española desde sus orígenes*, 1992, which should be used in conjunction with Catalán 2001). In between the *Leyenda de los Infantes de Lara* and the posthumously-published book that he left unfinished, he published — apart from a large number of articles — his *editio maior* of the *Cantar de Mio Cid* (1908–11), quickly followed by the *editio minor* with a quite different kind of introduction (1913), *L'épopée castillane à travers la littérature espagnole* (1910), *La España del Cid* (1929), *Historia y epopeya* (1934), *Reliquias de la poesía épica española* (1951), and *La 'Chanson de Roland' y el neotradicionalismo: orígenes de la épica románica* (1959) — eight books, most of them followed by revised or amplified editions. Partly because of his exceptional scholarly longevity and immense productivity, and partly, no doubt, because of the frequently observed phenomenon that owners come to resemble their dogs and, *mutatis mutandis*, scholars come to resemble their subject, Menéndez Pidal's work was often revised — 'vive en variantes y refundiciones'. Seventy-five years of research and reflection on the epic, years that saw a steady flow of editions, monographs, articles, and lectures — nearly twice the time that separates us from his death. It is not surprising that when Ernst Robert Curtius died at seventy Menéndez Pidal lamented the loss of 'este joven que todavía prometía tanto'.

---

[1]This was not his first major research project: his Madrid doctoral thesis was on the sources of *El Conde Lucanor* (Pérez Villanueva 1991: 56–57).

Menéndez Pidal's research and publications, though they cover so many subjects (as the programme for this Colloquium shows), form a coherent and organic whole: to take just two examples, his work on ballads is inextricably linked with his studies on the epic, and his hypothesis on the dating of the *Cantar de Mio Cid* both depends on and contributes to his work in historical linguistics. For that reason, any attempt to divide them into sections must to some extent falsify them, though if that attempt is not made any assessment of his work will lapse into incoherence. The same is, of course, true of any attempt to classify his work on the epic. Since readers can cope with false dichotomies more easily than with incoherence, I shall discuss each aspect of his epic studies separately: the general theory of neotraditionalism; the special theory of the multigeneric nature of Castilian epic material; his edition and studies (authorship, date, etc.) of the *Cantar de Mio Cid*; the hypothesis of Visigothic origins; and the recovery of the plots — and sometimes sections of verse — of lost epics from chronicles.

2. The general theory of neotraditionalism

The theory of neotraditionalism underlies not only all of Menéndez Pidal's work on the epic, but almost the whole of his research — literary, linguistic, and historical. It was not, of course, fully formulated at the outset, but developed gradually from a series of assumptions, often implicit rather than openly stated, to a coherent, impressive, enormously influential, and — as I have argued — flawed edifice. Concepts like neotraditionalism are seldom created *ex nihilo* by one scholar. Menéndez Pidal had predecessors, of whom the most important was Manuel Milá y Fontanals. When Menéndez Pidal was seventeen and in his first undergraduate year at the Universidad de Madrid, his elder brother Juan gave him a copy of Milá y Fontanals, *Poesía heroico-popular castellana*, which had been published twelve years earlier (Pérez Pascual 1998: 24).[2] Seldom can a gift have had such far-reaching consequences. It may well be that he would, sooner or later, have found his way to the research to which his whole adult

---

[2]Joaquín Pérez Villanueva says it was a loan (1991: 52). I do not know how to resolve this disagreement, but I provisionally accept Pérez Pascual's account, since the book would have been available to Menéndez Pidal in the university library, so a loan would hardly have been necessary.

life was dedicated, but that gift must, at the very least, have focussed his mind and given him a framework within which he could develop his ideas. He was later to credit Milá with responsibility for the theory of neotraditionalism, but its full development is undoubtedly his own. It may be summed up in his words:

> Otra teoría, que llamamos tradicionalística, piensa, en primer lugar, que el individuo más inventivo y genial no poetiza libérrimamente, sino que su genialidad actúa limitada y constreñida por la tradición cultural en que él se ha formado y a la cual él sirve. Pero, en segundo lugar, piensa que cuando un género literario se populariza en extremo (y éste es el caso de la epopeya), sus producciones están inmensamente más sujetas a la especial tradición de cultura en que aquel género se desarrolla; unos individuos colaboran habitualmente en la obra de otros, de manera que cada obra viene a tener una vida en cierto modo colectiva; la personalidad del autor, por relevante que sea, significa poco, tanto que pierde su propio nombre; el anónimo de las obras es rasgo fundamental, no es un mero acaso. (Menéndez Pidal 1992: 52)

Its tenets are presented in a number of his works, notably *Reliquias de la poesía épica española* (1951: vii–xiii), 'Problemas de la épica española' (1956), *Poesía juglaresca y orígenes de las literaturas románicas* (1957: chaps 13–14), and — extending the theory into French literature — *La 'Chanson de Roland' et la tradition épique des Francs* (1960: chap. 11).[3] The main elements of neotraditionalist theory may be summarized thus:

1. Castilian epic descends from Visigothic epic and thus, ultimately, from the oldest Germanic heroic poetry.

2. In the centuries that precede the earliest extant texts, the epic exists in a latent state, analogous to that of the pre-Roman words that are documented only towards the end of the Middle Ages.

3. The poems are born in the immediate aftermath of the events (see Menéndez Pidal 1992: 112–32).

4. The first version of a poem reflects historical reality, and fictional elements are in general the work of late revisers.

---

[3]Reactions by scholars in medieval French were, predictably, varied, but a favourable verdict came from Joseph J. Duggan: 'One of the notable achievements of [Roland] scholarship' (1976: 111).

5. The epic lives in variants and reworkings down the centuries and across genres.

6. Since chronicles prosify or summarize the texts of epics, they may be treated as direct witnesses in the reconstruction of lost epic texts and the editing of extant ones.

7. The poems are anonymous, not by chance but by their very nature, although this does not exclude the possibility of an individual poet, author of the first version.

8. The poets were lay minstrels, without interest in ecclesiastical matters; if such matters appear in the texts, they are late interpolations.[4]

A full account of neotraditionalist theory and of its history would fill a book — probably a long one —, but it is so well known that I think this summary, backed by a few quotations, will suffice. I shall devote most attention to the special theories summarized under 1, 5, 6, and 8, but before I turn to these I need to say something about the other four elements.

No. 2 does not seem to me to be controversial in its main contention. It would, of course, be rash to assume — as Menéndez Pidal often seemed to do — that every extant epic text was preceded by a long tradition of orally diffused versions; I have long believed (e.g. Deyermond 1982) that this was not the case with the *Cantar de Mio Cid*. Nevertheless, it would be very odd if Spain had never had a longish period of oral epic — odd both because of the evidence of epic tales in the chronicles (see section 5, below) and because most cultures have had, or in some cases still have, such a period. This is clearly documented by scholars such as H. Munro & N. Kershaw Chadwick (1932–40), C. M. Bowra (1950), Albert B. Lord (1960), and Arthur Hatto (1989).

Nos 3 and 4 are interdependent. Evidence for them is inevitably sparse, and I am not aware of any cases in the epic of other countries where a factual original is gradually interwoven with fictional elements: folk-motifs and other devices of fiction seem to play a large part throughout. In all of the Castilian epic legends that we can trace in chronicle and ballad, fictional elements seem to be strong from the

---

[4] This is a revised version of the list in Deyermond 1995: 48.

outset. Menéndez Pidal's opinion on this point has been attacked by a number of scholars, though defended by others. The most recent and thorough attack is the work of Eukene Lacarra Lanz (2005b), which uses a wide variety of historical sources to cast doubt on the veracity of the *Siete infantes de Lara*, on the existence of a number of versions, and on the early date (end of tenth century) proposed by Menéndez Pidal. Her argument on the first two points is convincing, but she never really gets to grips with Menéndez Pidal's case for early dating, despite frequent references to it in her article.

No. 7 (anonymity) is to a large extent true, and the question has not, as far as I know, been debated. It is, however, necessary to qualify the statement in two ways. First, this is not a peculiarly Spanish phenomenon: it is true of much Romance and Germanic poetry (and, to a lesser extent, prose) until the fourteenth century, though not of Latin. The three major exceptions are the Provençal troubadours, early Italian poets, and the Galician-Portuguese lyric poets. But these really are exceptions, and even when the fourteenth century is well advanced one of the greatest of Middle English poets is known only as the Gawain Poet. Secondly, in thirteenth-century Castile learned poets are generally anonymous: we know Berceo's name and something of his life, but we have two names (both disputed) for the *Libro de Alexandre*, and not a hint of the poet's identity for the *Libro de Apolonio*, the *Poema de Fernán González*, the *Vida de Santa María Egipciaca*, *¡Ay Jherusalem!*, *Razón de amor*, the debate poems, and so on. Anonymity is at this time peculiar neither to Spanish nor to popular literature. The time may have come for the question of anonymity to be looked at again, but it is clear that it should be deleted from the list of neotraditionalist features.

2.1 Visigothic origins

It would be hard to find today scholarly support for the hypothesis of Visigothic epic on Rodrigo and the Fall of Spain or on other subjects. Even Diego Catalán, eloquent and erudite defender of other parts of the neotraditionalist construct, did not believe in such epics: two sections of his book bear the titles 'No podemos testimoniar la existencia de temas épicos hispanos acudiendo a la Historiografía del s. XII' (2001: 238) and 'La imposible búsqueda de las raíces del género' (399). He says of the Fall of Spain:

> La [leyenda] de *El conde don Julián y la invasión musulmana* com-
> bina [...] componentes procedentes de la historiografía árabe
> (culpabilidad de Rodrigo, venganza de don Yllán, traición de
> los hijos de Vitiza, simulacro de canibalismo) con otros de
> origen cristiano (envío del conde a obrar las parias, consejo
> traidor de destruir las armas y de que los guerreros trabajen
> el campo, reunión de una asamblea en que se acepta ese
> consejo); la poesía épica no acudía a semejante tipo de fuentes
> ni contaba entre sus recursos con 'motivos' como los que
> desarrollan esas fuentes. (2001: 106n)

I am not convinced by the last statement: there is overwhelming
evidence of the presence of folk-motifs in epic (see Deyermond &
Chaplin 1972 and Goldberg in press). It would be extraordinary
if it were not so, given the way that such motifs pervade medieval
literature, even in learned forms such as the *exemplum* collection. But
the importance of Catalán's words derives not from that statement
but from what precedes it: all the elements of the tale of Rodrigo
and the Fall of Spain, best known to us in Pedro de Corral's *Crónica
sarracina* (Fogelquist 2001) are in readily accessible sources, and there
is no need to assume the existence of an epic poem. Catalán returns
to the subject:

> No puedo acompañarle [a Menéndez Pidal] en ninguna de
> éstas hipótesis: La primera leyenda referente a la conquista
> de España por invasores islamizados, me parece, en vista del
> conjunto de fuentes escritas que reunió el propio Menéndez
> Pidal (1925), de factura literaria árabe (aunque refleje tradi-
> ciones y pasiones de los *hispani* islamizados) (402)

It is worth noting that Victor Millet's excellent new book on Germanic
epic (2007), designed for Spanish readers, says nothing about a
hypothetical Visigothic epic. An *argumentum ex silentio* must, of
course, be treated with caution, but when the dog who did not bark in
the night leads us in the same direction as other evidence, he provides
useful confirmation. It is safe to conclude that there is no evidence
for a Visigothic epic in early medieval Spain, that the hypothesis of
its existence is unnecessary, and that this element of neotraditionalist
theory may be discarded.

2.2 The multigeneric nature of Castilian epic material

This concept was not new: even the least attentive reader would have noticed Guillén de Castro's *Las mocedades del Cid* or ballads on epic subjects. Yet a general awareness of the presence of epic material in late-medieval, Golden Age, and Romantic literature did not take clear and coherent form until Menéndez Pidal was invited to give the Turnbull Lectures at Johns Hopkins University in March 1909, and chose as his subject an aspect of Spanish literature that sharply differentiated it from other Western European literatures. These do indeed make use of epic (Wagner's *Der Ring des Nibelungen*, written in 1853, for example, or his *Siegfried*, performed in 1876), but infrequently: where is the Elizabethan play of Beowulf? And the hero of by far the best known classic French play on an epic subject is not Roland or Guillaume d'Orange but the Cid. The Turnbull Lectures, published in French in 1910 (thirty-five years passed before the appearance of the Spanish version, 1945) were highly, and rightly, influential. Once Menéndez Pidal had marshalled his evidence and set out his argument, there was no dispute. The uniquely multigeneric nature of Castilian epic material became part of the common currency of medieval studies.[5]

2.3 The recovery of lost epics from chronicles

Menéndez Pidal's reputation in epic studies was made almost over-night by the publication of *La leyenda de los infantes de Lara* in 1896. He continued to work on this subject, in the intervals of other projects, throughout his life, but saw no reason to undertake major revision, for he remained convinced of the validity of both his methods and his conclusions. The changes that he made in the second edition, published in 1934, and in some separate studies were additions, not reworkings, as may be seen in the posthumous third edition of 1971, an edition that, like so much else, was made possible by the devoted work of Diego Catalán. Catalán reprints the first edition in its entirety, and adds all subsequent work on the *Siete infantes* that Menéndez Pidal ever published, arranging the material in chronological layers and adding an invaluable index (without

---

[5]The phenomenon was still noticeable throughout Menéndez Pidal's life, and has continued after his death: see, for example, Sanmateu 1997 on the Cid in the cinema.

it, adequate consultation of this invaluable book would have been almost impossible). One of the two most notable features of this first book is the establishment of relations between the story of the Infantes de Lara as told in chronicles (chiefly in the Alfonsine tradition) and archival documents. The other is the use of those chronicles as direct witnesses to the lost text of the poem, enabling Menéndez Pidal to reconstruct not just isolated lines of verse but whole sections of the lost poem. As time went by the number of reconstructed lines rose, partly because of the use of new chronicle sources and partly because of his increasing confidence in the technique. It rose from about 350 in the first edition (1896) to some 600 in *Reliquias* (1951). This has proved to be one of the most controversial aspects of Menéndez Pidal's work, partly because not all scholars agree that a chronicle can be treated as a direct witness, partly because of the element of conjectural emendation in some of the reconstructed lines, but largely because his reconstructed sections mix lines from different chronicles (see Alberto Montaner's cautionary words, 1993b). Some of those who have written about the reconstruction of lost lines from chronicles have, I think, been too sceptical, too narrow in their definition of a direct witness. It is true that lines of verse may spontaneously get into prose (I have noticed that those writing extensively about the *Laberinto de Fortuna* quite often, though unconsciously, write phrases and sentences in a perfect *arte mayor* rhythm), but these are isolated cases, and are in no way comparable to the passages of verse detected by Menéndez Pidal. Moreover, this phenomenon is not, as far as I know, found in medieval English, French, or German chronicles. The discovery of such passages remains, therefore, one of Menéndez Pidal's enduring successes.[6]

Nevertheless, the mixture of lines from different chronicles is difficult to reconcile with Menéndez Pidal's belief that the chronicles provide evidence for at least two versions of the *Siete infantes*. It

---

[6]Two papers read at the conferences of the Association of Hispanists of Great Britain and Ireland, one by Keith Whinnom and the other by Jane Whetnall, argued for the priority of the chronicle texts: the story of the Siete Infantes, for instance, first took coherent narrative shape in the chronicles, and any verse narratives derived from these. It may be significant that neither scholar chose to publish the paper (Whinnom later said that his was, to some extent, written tongue-in-cheek).

seems to me that there is evidence for two versions of this poem, and of the lost *Cantar de Sancho II*, but that we cannot rely on an eclectic reconstruction of whole passages, and it is on balance unfortunate that passages reconstructed in this way have passed into general currency through books such as Alvar & Alvar 1991: 175–270, so that students and general readers may — despite the words of caution on p. 178 — believe that they have in their hands an authentic poetic text preserved since the Middle Ages.

2.4 Lay minstrels, not ecclesiastical or other learned poets

Menéndez Pidal was never in doubt about this. Two quotations illustrate his view: 'La epopeya era la poesía de los caballeros, y no se preocupaba gran cosa de los hombres de iglesia' (1934: 97), and 'La inspiración de los cantares es caballeresca, no eclesiástica; juglaresca, no clerical, contra lo que pretende Bédier para la épica francesa' (1944–46: III, 1171). These statements must be tested against the available evidence, and any substantial incompatibility between hypothesis and observed data requires modification of the hypothesis. It does not matter if there are data that support the hypothesis: it is the negative evidence that counts. Such evidence is plentiful in a poem that Menéndez Pidal studied, on and off, for more than half a century: from an article on ballads about Fernán González (1899) to his *Romancero hispánico* (1953): I refer, of course, to the *Mocedades de Rodrigo*. I have summarized and discussed his opinions in my *Mocedades* book (1969: 44–46), and there is no need to go over the ground again. I need say only that a careful reading of the *Cantar de Mio Cid* also provides strong evidence against the hypothesis, and that even those scholars who are most sympathetic to the neotraditionalist approach now accept the need to modify Menéndez Pidal's opinion on this matter.

Menéndez Pidal worked on all of the extant epics — *Roncesvalles*, which he discovered and edited, and the *Poema de Fernán González*, as well as the *Cantar de Mio Cid* and the *Mocedades de Rodrigo* — and on most of the lost ones. It would be impossible, even in an article twice as long as this, to give an adequate account of his work on these poems, let alone a survey of reactions to it. What I have said in section 2.3, above, will have to serve as a token recognition of his work on lost epics, and I shall now turn to his research on the *Cantar de Mio*

Cid, spread over more than seventy years.

3. The editing of the *Cantar de Mio Cid*

As with the general theory of neotraditionalism and its component elements, I need to separate into misleadingly neat and tidy compartments aspects of Menéndez Pidal's work on the *Cantar*. We must not forget, however, that his studies of language, date, and place are fundamental to his conjectural emendations of the text, as is his study of the *Cantar*'s relation to the chronicles. And the aspects of his study of the text that we need to discuss separately — and that he sets out separately in the introductions both to his *editio maior* of 1908–11 and to the *editio minor* of 1913 — are mutually supportive: date is, for example, related to language, transmission, and historicity. This is, of course, true to some extent of all research, and Leo Spitzer's concept of the 'philological circle' (see Catano 1988: 129–36) has become famous, but Menéndez Pidal's circle is both larger and more complex, because it includes, as a major element, the process of editing.

The structure and to some extent the content of Menéndez Pidal's *editio maior* are, even three decades later in the second edition, influenced to an astonishing degree by the conditions of the Real Academia's 1892 competition. He says in his 1908 preface:

> Entretanto, se completaban mis estudios sobre las Crónicas, tan necesarias para la crítica del Cantar; mis ideas sobre la métrica de éste cambiaban radicalmente […], y mi conocimiento de la toponimia del poema se ensanchaba, con ayuda de excursiones sobre el terreno; de modo que, cada año que pasaba, me era más difícil poner mi anticuada obra al corriente de las nuevas publicaciones ajenas y de las nuevas ideas propias.
>
> Por fin ahora sale a luz mi trabajo, refundido completamente, *pero sin alteración en el primitivo plan, ni siquiera en el número y contenido de los párrafos en que al comienzo lo dividí.* (1944–46: I, ix–x; my italics)

So only on metrics did Menéndez Pidal's opinion change significantly between 1892 and 1908; everything else was expansion and modification at the edges of the topic. And for half a century after he began his work on the text his opinions remained essentially unchanged, as he explains in the preface to the second edition: 'el tiempo y el gusto para refundir [la edición] me faltaba siempre, porque no hallaba nada esencial en que hubiera de alterarla' (1954–56: I, v).[7]

It is not surprising that some of the opinions formed at the end of the nineteenth century should, at the beginning of the twenty-first, be widely regarded as mistaken, and that others, while accepted in general terms, should be disputed in detail. What is surprising — and a testimony to Menéndez Pidal's quality as a scholar — is that so much of his thought about the *Cantar* is still generally accepted.

The task of an editor of the *Cantar* is in one way much easier than that of most editors, but in another way more difficult. The ease and the difficulty have the same cause: the unique manuscript. Manuals of textual criticism do not usually have much to say about the problems of editing a work that survives in a single witness. I have looked at the five that I possess — one devoted to Middle English, one to Old French, and three, explicitly or implicitly, to Castilian.[8] It is not altogether surprising that the manual on French offers little help on this matter, because relatively few Old French texts survive in a unique manuscript, but Middle English has a fair number of such texts, and they are frequent in medieval Castilian, so the reticence of these manuals is regrettable. There is, of course, no problem if the editor offers a paleographic edition: all that is necessary is a clear eye and a steady hand. But a critical edition is another matter. As Menéndez Pidal said,

> El poema del Cid ofrece uno de los casos más difíciles que en
> la crítica de un texto pueden presentarse, ya que se conserva

---

[7]Towards the end of his life Menéndez Pidal made a radical change in his view of the poem's authorship, attributing it to two poets, one from San Esteban de Gormaz (c.1105) and the other from Medinaceli, who, c.1140, reworked and expanded the poem inherited from his predecessor (Menéndez Pidal 1961). His new opinion, widely accepted at the time because of his unrivalled authority, does not now carry much weight (for a brief account of its weaknesses, see Deyermond 1977: 20). The 1961 article was to a large extent an attempt to explain conflicting evidence on the date of the poem; Diego Catalán says that 'creo que sus nuevas ideas tuvieron como base fundamental un razonamiento circular' (2001: 443).

[8]Moorman 1975, Foulet & Speer 1979, Blecua 1983, Fradejas Rueda 1991, and Pérez Priego 2001.

en un solo manuscrito, muy posterior a la fecha de la obra e infiel al estado primitivo de la misma. De aquí la gran divergencia de criterio que se observa entre los que han trabajado sobre la reconstrucción del texto. (1944–46: III, 1017)

I do not entirely agree with the reasons that he gives, but there is no doubt that his conclusion is correct: the unique manuscript of the *Cantar* does indeed present an unusually difficult case. A colleague whom I consulted, an expert on codicology, thought there was nothing odd in the manuals' neglect of the single witness, since its editing is straightforward. That is undoubtedly true of many works, but Menéndez Pidal is right about the *Cantar*.

In dealing with a work whose single witness is both incomplete and at a distance from the original, editors have just two tools at their disposal, conjectural emendation and indirect witnesses. Menéndez Pidal discusses these in chapter 3, 'Recursos emendatorios aplicables al códice único', of 1944–46. The bases that he uses for emendation are the place of composition (I, 34–76), metre (76–103), assonance patterns (103–24), and the evidence of the chronicles (124–36). There is one conspicuous absence: the date of composition. This is discussed in an earlier section (I, 19–28), but since it is the basis for very many of Menéndez Pidal's emendations its use as an editorial tool should have been examined along with place, metre, etc.

Both date and place of composition need to be handled with extreme care as bases for emendation, since they are –– even more than other aspects of textual criticism –– likely to produce circular arguments. If there were clear external evidence for the place and the time at which the *Cantar* was composed, there would be a secure base for the editor, but all the evidence is internal. The editor may (and Menéndez Pidal often does) fall into the trap of dating the poem by linguistic features, emending the language to fit the date, and using the emended language as evidence for that date.

Textual criticism, like almost every human activity, is subject to fashion. Thirty years ago I wrote that

the extrovert, optimistic nineteenth century, believing in self-improvement, the perfectibility of human nature and human institutions, and the inevitability of progress, was under-standably confident of its ability to reconstitute the perfect text. Today, battered by world wars, economic crises and the decline of the West, undermined by Freud's revelations and by the retreat from religion, we look more suspiciously on our textual intuitions, and hold more tightly to the security of the extant MS. (1977: 17n6)

That, of course, refers to conjectural emendation, not to Lachmannian textual criticism applied to a work with a number of witnesses, but what I said applies, *mutatis mutandis*, to the editing of a text with only one direct witness, and all editors in the past quarter-century have been much more cautious than Menéndez Pidal in their conjectural emendation. We should recall that — odd though it may now seem — Menéndez Pidal regarded himself as in some respects a conservative editor:

En la edición crítica [...] me aparto de la mayoría de los eruditos, adoptando un criterio más conservador que el de ellos en cuanto a las lecciones del códice único, y más innovador en cuanto a las asonancias y a las formas de lenguaje. Tanto se peca por quitar y poner palabras en cada verso del manuscrito único, usando de una libertad injustificada, como por no restaurar el arcaísmo oportuno, cayendo en una timidez o negligencia no estimuladas siquiera por la llamativa falta de la rima ('Advertencia a la edición de 1908'; 1944–46: I, x)[9]

In one sense, then, Smith, Michael, and Montaner may be seen as continuing a process that he had begun.

Time plays tricks with the memory, and I have more than once been surprised, on looking again at Menéndez Pidal's critical edition side by side with that of Smith or Michael, at how much they have in common. There is no space to give a detailed comparative account of Menéndez Pidal's *editio maior* and the principal editions published since his death: those of Smith, Michael, Horrent, Montaner, and Funes. Fortunately, most of that work has been done in the magisterial article by Germán Orduna (1997). As minimal illustration, I

---

[9]As Leonardo Funes says, 'lo que a principios del siglo XX podía percibirse como una postura conservadora con respecto al manuscrito, para nuestros actuales criterios representa una disposición ampliamente enmendatoria' (2007: ci). For the long series of published editions, Tomás Antonio Sánchez's *Colección de poesías castellanas anteriores al siglo XV*, begun in 1779, see Deyermond 1997.

give in the Appendix two samples of text, the first of which shows substantial agreement between Menéndez Pidal and later editors (only three lines out of ten show differences), while the second shows fundamental disagreement, with Menéndez Pidal's addition of a line on the basis of a chronicle passage (see section 3.4, below).[10]

I had intended to look in detail at the most important bases for Menéndez Pidal's conjectural emendations: metre, date, and place. Having done so in the second draft of this paper, I have come to realize that detailed coverage of these questions requires far more space than is available, and that it is in any case unnecessary. I shall, therefore, say briefly what seems to me to be the present state of opinion, and how it differs from Pidalian orthodoxy. Before I do so, however, I should acknowledge that opinion on these matters in Spain during the years of Menéndez Pidal's dominance was not as monolithic as it seemed from outside (or, indeed, as it seemed to most Spanish readers of the *Cantar*). For many years some scholars working in Spain dissented from Pidalian orthodoxy, but their voices were seldom heard outside a small circle (Colin Smith, in his 1992 article, gives a fascinating and bibliographically rich account of this dissent between the completion of Menéndez Pidal's *editio maior* in 1911 and his death in 1968).

3.1. Metre

As we have seen, metre is the only area in which Menéndez Pidal changed his opinion significantly between the 1892 competition and the publication of the *editio maior*. He came to realize that the poem could not be edited on metrical evidence, because of the extreme difficulty of understanding its metre: he refers to 'una versificación primitiva irregular ajustada a leyes totalmente desconocidas para

---

[10]The edition by Juan Carlos Bayo and Ian Michael, published as I was writing the last pages of this article, is the third edition of Michael's Clásicos Castalia edition, first published in 1975. This was intended by the editors to be a major revision and expansion, to rival Montaner 2007, but the sale of Castalia to a conglomerate has had a disastrous effect on its publishing policy, and the new edition has been shorn of its apparatus criticus and bibliography, and almost all of its introduction. Fortunately, the indispensable 75-page 'índice onomástico' has survived, and the text is the result of the editors' extensive revision. In the lines that I have chosen for comparison, the orthographic conventions have been changed (*ý* and *nn* are preserved, instead of being modernized as *í* and *ñ*), but there are no substantive differences.

nosotros' (1908–11: I, 83), and concludes that 'Como consecuencia de la irregularidad métrica del Cantar de Mio Cid, concluiremos la poca utilidad que el metro tiene para sugerir correcciones al texto.' (103). This was a prudent decision, because scholarly opinion on the metre has been changed radically in the last decade by Juan Carlos Bayo's doctoral thesis (1999) and then Martin Duffell's research:

> The number of stresses per hemistich in the poem is much more constant than the number of syllables: by any definition of a stress, a clear majority of hemistichs (60 per cent of both first and second) contain two, and 95 per cent contain either two or three. (Duffell 2007: 77)

> The surviving text provides ample evidence that the *PMC*'s poet did not count syllables or moras, nor did he count accents in the slavish way his French contemporaries counted syllables. The text we have shows that he counted pairs of phrases, and emphasized this by assonance closing the second of each pair. The foregoing analysis also strongly suggests that he counted beats in very much the same way as Old and Middle English poets. (80–81)

In the light of this development, it would not be particularly useful to survey the opinions of the editors on the metre of the *Cantar*, though I should note that Alberto Montaner's pages on the subject (2007: clxx–clxxix) are of great interest.

3.2. Date

As is well known, the Pidalian consensus on the poem's chronology — composition around 1140 — was broken in 1952 by Peter Russell's article; more accurately, it should have been broken, yet in Spain and America the article was, to a degree that now seems inconceivable, ignored. When the article was published in Spanish translation in 1978, however, the transformation was as spectacular as it was sudden.[11]

There is, of course, still widespread acceptance of an early date of composition, partly because of unawareness of developments in research, and partly because some scholars — perhaps more in the

---

[11]On the lack of response, see the comments by Juan Carlos Bayo (2002: 15–17) and Peter Russell (2002: 68–69).

United States than in Spain — have considered the arguments for composition at the beginning of the thirteenth century and found them unconvincing. Yet the most influential recent editors favour late composition. Alberto Montaner writes:

> En suma, no se trata de elementos aislados que pudieran deberse a una intercalación o a una reelaboración parcial, sino de un cúmulo de aspectos consustanciales al Cantar en todos sus niveles y que, al margen de posibles antecedentes en forma poética, conducen a fecharlo con apenas dudas en las cercanías de 1200. (2007: lxxix)

Leonardo Funes is more cautious, but concludes: 'considero que los argumentos que sostienen una fecha más tardía tienen mayor peso' (2007: xv).

3.3. Place

Several questions have been discussed (and sometimes confused). Where was the poet born? Where did he live and work? What was his dialect? Menéndez Pidal's belief (until his late conversion to the two-poet hypothesis: see n7, above) was that the poet came from Medinaceli, an origin revealed in the dialect of the text, the detailed accounts of events in that area (in contrast to the brief narration of the conquest of Valencia), and the detailed topography. This view has worn better than his conclusions on date and metre. British scholars have in general argued for composition by a Burgos poet. Thus, for instance, Ralph Penny concludes his study of the *Cantar*'s language with the words:

> there are some reasons for preferring Burgos, or its immediate vicinity, as the place of origin of the author, rather than Medinaceli / Soria, despite the familiarity of the author with the geography of the latter region. (2002: 100)

Diego Catalán takes the contrary view. The pages that he dedicates to this subject (not known to Penny when he wrote his paper) are few but important (2001: 436–39). The points that he makes are essentially those made by Menéndez Pidal, but he has thought carefully about them and he presents his results cogently. For instance:

creo que, si poseyéramos el antígrafo del que se sacó la copia
de Vivar, la lengua del Mio Cid nos sorprendería por su lejanía
respecto a los patrones burgaleses del castellano, toda vez
que, a lo que parece, ese prototipo conservaba con fidelidad
los rasgos lingüísticos de un arquetipo 'extremadano', cuya
existencia más adelante defenderé. (439)

Funes agrees that at least the poet lived in the city, even if he was
not born there (2007: xviii). Montaner's judicious survey, based
on wide reading of scholarly opinions since 1970 on the identity of
the poet and his origin (2007: lxvi–lxxi), concludes that 'no resultan
válidos ninguno de los argumentos de identificación concreta del
autor propuestos hasta ahora ni la mayoría de los razonamientos de
localización' (lxxi).

3.4. Relation to chronicles

The treatment of chronicle prosifications as direct witnesses is one
of the major elements of neotraditionalist theory (see section 2.3,
above). The most obvious effect of this treatment on the editing of
the Cantar is the provision, chiefly from the *Crónica de Castilla*, of
narrative that precedes the first line of the extant manuscript (see
Armistead 1983–84 and Montaner 1995). The most interesting case,
however — the one that brings the methodological question into
sharpest focus —, is the addition by Menéndez Pidal (followed by
Jules Horrent but not by the other editors) of 'mas a grand ondra
tornaremos a Castiella' after line 14. The extra line, taken from
the chronicles, explains the Cid's words '¡Albricia, Álbar Fáñez,
ca echados somos de tierra!'. But, as most editors recognize, the
explanation is unnecessary: the poet's meaning is clear. Despite
Samuel Armistead's powerful advocacy (1989), I am convinced that
we are here confronted by the difference between the chronicler's
and the poet's cast of mind. The chronicler's task is to remove any
uncertainty, while the poet, having pointed his audience in the right
direction, leaves it at that. There is an analogous case in the editing of
English poetry: Richard Bentley, the editor of Manilius, described by
A. E. Housman as 'the greatest scholar that England or perhaps that
Europe ever bred', decided to edit *Paradise Lost,* and brought to the
task the assumptions as well as the skills formed in decades of work

on classical Latin.[12] The result was a series of editorial decisions that have been a source of merriment ever since, because Bentley made explicit and prosaic lines in which Milton had implied a meaning (see White 1965: chap. 22).

There is no scholarly consensus on the general issue of the use of chronicles as direct witnesses of the *Cantar*, but there is a clear consensus on the two specific instances to which I have referred: with Menéndez Pidal in the first case, against him in the second.

4. Historicity

Menéndez Pidal was convinced from a very early stage in his re-search that the *Cantar* is an accurate historical record: the section on 'Elementos ficticios' in the introduction to his 1913 edition deals only with the episodes of Raquel and Vidas, the escaped lion, and (oddly, since it is the one incident incapable of proof or disproof) the appearance of the archangel Gabriel. Here one aspect of his opinions, concerned with the historicity of the action, has fared badly because it is based on an *a priori* belief, whereas his conclusions on the historicity of many of the minor characters — conclusions based on long and careful archival research — command universal respect.

A case that merits special attention is that of the hero's social rank. Menéndez Pidal had no doubt that the historical Rodrigo Díaz was, like the Cid of the poem, an *infanzón*, a member of the lower ranks of the nobility. This opinion was one that, for a very long time, we all accepted unhesitatingly. Even Smith and Michael, ready to challenge Menéndez Pidal on the general historicity of the poem as well as on editorial method, did not challenge him here: 'The Cid was born in about 1040 in a family of *infanzones*, one of the lower ranks of the nobility' (Smith 1972: xxv), and 'Born into the rank of *infanzón* (or baronet) […]' (Michael et al. 1975: 1). But, astonishingly, none of us noticed that Menéndez Pidal, far from having documentary evidence

---

[12]Housman's words are quoted from his Introductory Lecture given in 1892 (Housman 1961: 12). He goes on: 'Bentley was born in the year 1662, and he brought with him into the world […] a prosaic mind; nor did all his immense study of the classics avail to confer on him a true appreciation of poetry. While he dealt with the classical poets he was relatively safe, for in dealing with these a prosaic mind is not so grave a disqualification as a dithyrambic mind', but the effects on his editing of Milton were catastrophic, as Housman's quotations (1961: 12–13) show.

for the historical Cid's social status, had assumed that what was true of the poetic hero was true of the eleventh-century man. It was an *a priori* assumption, a special case of the wider hypothesis of the poem's extreme historicity. Historians were, naturally, more cautious than literary scholars in their approach to this question. Richard Fletcher, for example, says of the historical Rodrigo Díaz:

> His family was aristocratic. […] It is indeed true that he did remarkably well for himself, but the home-base from which he set out was not a humble one. The earliest piece of writing about Rodrigo, the […] *Carmen Campi Doctoris*, says of his ancestry:
>
>> Nobiliori de genere ortus,
>> Quo in castella non est illo maius,
>
> which may be literally translated: 'He is sprung from a more noble family, there is none older than it in Castile.' The phrasing is curious. In an age when distinguished ancestry was rated highly, this would seem to be a polite way of saying that Rodrigo did not belong to the topmost ranks of the aristocracy. (1989: 107–08)

There the matter remained until about ten years ago, when some Spanish historians began to look more closely at the documentary evidence on the hero's family. Eukene Lacarra Lanz has reassessed the question in detail, evaluating the findings of the historians and coming to a startling conclusion: 'Así vemos que Rodrigo, lejos de ser un simple infanzón, estaba excelentemente emparentado con todas las monarquías hispanas' (2005a: 124; see also 2007). Her case for seeing the historical Cid in a new light is irresistible, but, astonishingly, she has fallen in …to the same error as Menéndez Pidal, though approaching it from the opposite direction. C. S. Lewis, for many years a Fellow of this college, said that humans have an odd way of reacting to error: having fallen off a horse on one side, they try correct the error by falling off on the other side. Menéndez Pidal believed that because the Cid is presented in the poem as an *infanzón*, he must have been one in real life. Lacarra Lanz believes that because the historical Cid was of much higher rank, the hero of the poem must have been presented as a high noble. This is not how I read the text.

5. Criticism

The bibliography that I distributed in my course on the *Cantar* in Madrid last November contains just under 100 entries that are wholly or in large measure devoted to literary criticism of the poem (this is, of course, a selection, which includes only those that I think worthy of attention). Three are books, the remainder articles or chapters in books. Checking, for the first time, the geographical origin of these studies, I found to my astonishment that three-quarters are from the United Kingdom and North America (UK 37, USA 35, Canada 3). Only fifteen are from Spain; no other country has more than two. These cannot, of course, be exact figures: when a scholar moves from one country to another, we can seldom know where the study began. But the results are so clear that no possible margin of error can seriously affect them. How can we account for this disparity? I wonder if the long shadow of Menéndez Pidal — despite the excellent example set by Dámaso Alonso in 1941 — may have inhibited his successors (even those who disagree with him)?

The introduction to Menéndez Pidal's *editio minor* — the form in which, for over sixty years, the great majority of readers first encountered the *Cantar* — devotes only a small proportion of its 109 pages to literary matters: 13 pages on 'Valor artístico' and 4 on 'Olvidos del juglar'. Even if we add the 5 pages of plot summary, that is only one-fifth of the introduction. 'Valor histórico y arqueológico', by contrast, occupies 25 pages, with 21 on 'Difusión y éxito' and 13 on 'Elemento histórico'. Not until eighty years after Menéndez Pidal's *editio minor*, did a Spanish editor break with this tradition: out of 95 pages of introduction to Alberto Montaner's first edition (1993a), 74 are on literary matters. Montaner's example proved decisive: when Juan Carlos Conde was asked to produce Menéndez Pidal's edition in a new form for Colección Austral (1999), he devoted 17 pages of a 42-page introduction to literary aspects. Almost half of Leonardo Funes's introduction to his edition (2007) deals with versification, structure, ideology, and similar topics. In the much amplified version of Montaner's edition, published in 2007, two-thirds of the introduction is concerned with literary criticism, and most of the rest with textual criticism; there is not a mention of archaeological value or most of the other questions that preoccupied

Menéndez Pidal.[13] I hope that the predominance of literary criticism in these editions — as well as, of course, in those by Smith and Michael — will stimulate young scholars in Spain and Latin America to devote more books and articles to the *Cantar*'s literary qualities (and, indeed, its defects).

6. Conclusion

I said at the outset that Menéndez Pidal is still a living force in epic scholarship. Let me conclude by offering meteorological corroboration of this judgment. I should warn readers that what I am about to say strains credulity, but it is literally true; I have not invented, I have not embellished. Thirty-nine years ago, a few months after Menéndez Pidal's death, I was lecturing on the *Cantar de Mio Cid* at Westfield. It was a beautiful spring day: sun, clear and cloudless sky, a gentle breeze. It was time to discuss the date of composition of the *Cantar*, and I presented the arguments on both sides, concluding that c. 1207 was the most likely date. 'Of course', I said, 'Menéndez Pidal would strongly disagree, but he's now unable to say so.' Immediately, out of that clear English sky, came a flash of lightning and a thunderclap. 'Sorry, sir', I said.

Appendix
Case A

MS:	Hy gaño a colada q*ue* mas vale de mill marcos de plata	1010
MPp:	Hy gaño a Colada q*ue* mas vale de mill marcos de plata.	
SA:	Hy ganó à Colada que mas vale de mill marcos de plata.	(1018)
MPc:	hi gañó a Colada que más vale de mill <u>marcos</u>.	em
SM:	Hi gaño a Colada, que mas vale de mill marcos de plata,	
MI:	Í gañó a Colada, que más vale de mill marcos de plata.	
HO:	Hy gaño a Colada, q*ue* más vale de mill marcos de plata,	
MO:	_gañó a Colada, que más vale de mill marcos de plata,	
FU:	_gañó a Colada, que más vale de mil marcos de plata,	

---

[13]The one defect of this splendid edition is the brevity of the table of contents. I have constructed my own detailed table, and I suspect that many other readers have done the same.

MS: [Y ben]ç[io] eſta batalla poro ondro ſu barba   /1011/
MPp: [Y ben]ç[io] eſta batalla poro ōndro ſu barba,
SA: E venció esta batalla poró ondro su barba.
MPc: I venció esta batalla por o ondró su barba,
SM: i bençio esta batalla por o ondro su barba;
MI: [Í bençió] esta batalla por ó ondró su barba.
HO: y bencio esta batalla, por o ondró su barba.
MO: _benció esta batalla, por o ondró su barba.
FU: _bençió esta batalla, por o ondró su barba.

MS: Priſo lo al conde pora ſu tierra lo leuaua   /1012/
MPp: Priſo lo al conde, pora ſu tierra lo leuaua,
SA: Prísolo al Conde, pora su tienda lo lebaba:
MPc: prísolo al comde, pora su tienda lo levava;
SM: priso lo al conde, pora su tie[nd]a lo levava,
MI: Prísolo al conde, pora su tienda lo levava,
HO: Priso lo al conde, pora su tie[nd]a lo leuaua,
MO: Prísolo al conde, pora su tienda lo levava,
FU: Prísolo al conde, pora su tie[nd]a lo levava;

MS: Aſos creenderos <u>mandar lo guardaua</u>   1013
MPp: Aſos creenderos <u>mandar lo guardaua</u>.
SA: A sus Creenderos <u>mandarlo guardaba</u>.
MPc: a sos creenderos guardar lo mandava.   em
SM: a sos creenderos guardar lo mandava.
MI: a sos creenderos guardarlo mandava.
HO: a sos creenderos guardar lo mandaua.
MO: a sos creenderos guardarlo mandava.
FU: a sos creenderos [guardarlo mandava].

MS: De fuera dela tienda vn ſalto daua   /1014/
MPp: De fuera dela tienda vn ſalto daua,
SA: De fuera de la tienda un salto daba.
MPc: De fuera de la tienda un salto dava,
SM: De fuera de la tienda un salto dava,
MI: De fuera de la tienda un salto dava,
HO: De fuera de la tienda vn salto daua,
MO: De fuera de la tienda un salto dava,
FU: De fuera de la tienda un salto dava,

MS: De todas partes los ſos ſe <u>aiuntaron</u>   1015
MPp: De todas partes los ſos ſe <u>aiuntaron</u>;
SA: De todas partes los sos se <u>aïuntaron</u>.
MPc: de todas partes los sos se ajunta*van*;   em
SM: de todas partes los sos se ajunta[va]n;
MI: de todas partes los sos se <u>aiuntaron</u>;
HO: de todas partes los sos se aiunta[ua]n;
MO: de todas partes los sos se ayuntavan;
FU: de todas partes los sos se ayunta[va]n.

MS: Plogo a myo cid, ca grandes ſon las ganançias   /1016/
MPp: Plogo a myo Çid, ca grandes ſon las ganançias.
SA: Plógo à mio Cid, ca grandes son las ganancias.
MP: plogo a mio Çid, ca grandes son las ganançias.
SM: plogo a mio Çid ca grandes son las ganançias.
MI: plogo a Mio Çid ca grandes son las ganançias.
HO: plogo a myo Çid ca grandes son las ganançias.
MO: plogo a mio Cid ca grandes son las ganancias.
FU: Plogo a mio Çid, ca grandes son las ganançias.

MS: A my*o* Cid don Rodrigo grant cozinal adobaua*n*   /1017/
MPp: A myo Çid don Rodrigo grant cozinal adobaua*n*;
SA: A mio Cid Don Rodrigo grant cocinal' adobaban:
MPc: A mio Çid don Rodrigo grant cozínal adobavan;
SM: A mio Çid don Rodrigo grant cozinal adobavan;
MI: A mio Çid don Rodrigo grant cozínal' adobavan;
HO: A myo Çid don RRodrigo grant cozinal adobaua*n*;
MO: A mio Cid don Rodrigo grant cozina l'adobavan,
FU: A mio Çid don Rodrigo grant cozinal adobavan,

MS: El conde don Remont non gelo pre*çia nada   /1018/
MPp: El conde don Remont non gelo pre*çia nada,
SA: El Conde Don Remont non gelo precia nada.
MPc: el conde don Remont non gelo preçia nada;
SM: el conde don Remont non gelo preçia nada,
MI: el conde don Remont non ge lo preçia nada,
HO: el conde don RRemont non gelo preçia nada,
MO: el conde don Remont non ge lo precia nada;
FU: el conde don Remont non ge lo preçia nada.

MS:	Aduzen le los comeres delant gelos parauan	/1019/
MPp:	Aduzen le los comeres, delant gelos parauan;	
SA:	Aducenle los comeres, delante gelos paraban:	(1027)
MPc:	adúzenle los comeres, delant gelos paravan,	
SM:	aduzen le los comeres, delant gelos paravan,	
MI:	adúzenle los comeres, delant ge los paravan,	
HO:	aduzen le los comeres, delant gelos parauan,	
MO:	adúzenle los comeres, delant ge los paravan,	
FU:	Adúzenle los comeres, delant ge los paravan,	

Case B

MS:	Albricia Albarffanez ca echados fomos de tierra	14
MPp:	'Albricia Albarffanez, ca echados fomos de tierra!'	
SA:	'Albrizias Alvar Fanez ca echados somos de tierra'	
MPc:	'albricia, Álbar Fáñez, ca echados somos de-tierra!	
	Mas a grand ondra tornaremos a Castiella.'	em
SM:	'¡Albriçia, Albar Ffanez, ca echados somos de tierra!'	
MI:	'¡Albriçia, Álbar Fáñez, ca echados somos de tierra!'	
HO:	'¡Albriçia, Albar Ffanez, ca echados somos de tierra!	
	Mas a gran ondra tornar nos hemos a Castiella.'	
MO:	'¡Albricia, Álbar Fáñez, ca echados somos de tierra!'	
FU:	'¡Albriçia Álbar Fáñez, ca echados somos de tierra!'	

Key:

MS	Facsimile (Burgos, 1988)
MPp	Menéndez Pidal's paleographic edition (1944–46)
SA	Thomás Antonio Sánchez's edition (1779)
MPc	Menéndez Pidal's critical edition (1944–46)
SM	Colin Smith's edition (1976)
MI	Ian Michael's edition (1978)
HO	Jules Horrent's edition (1982)
MO	Alberto Montaner's edition (2007)
FU	Leonardo Funes's edition (2007)
/1011/	No significant difference in this line between MS and any of the editions.
marcos.	Differs from the consensus.
em	emendation by Menéndez Pidal.

Works Cited

ALONSO, Dámaso, 1941. 'Estilo y creación en el *Poema del Cid'*, *Escorial*, 3: 333–72. Repr. in his *Ensayos sobre poesía española* (Madrid: Revista de Occidente, 1944), pp. 69–111.

ALVAR, Carlos , & Manuel ALVAR , ed., 1991. *Épica medieval española*, Letras Hispánicas, 330 (Madrid: Cátedra).

ARMISTEAD, Samuel G., 1983–84. 'The Initial Verses of the *Cantar de Mio Cid'*, *C*, 12: 178–86.

——, 1989. 'Cantares de gesta y crónicas alfonsíes: "Mas a grand ondra / tornaremos a Castiella"', in *Actas del IX Congreso de la Asociación Internacional de Hispanistas* (Berlín, agosto de 1986), ed. Sebastian Neumeister (Frankfurt am Main: Vervuert), I, pp. 177–85.

BAYO, Juan Carlos, 1999. 'La teoría del verso desde el punto de vista lingüístico: el sistema de versificación del *Cantar de Mio Cid'*, doctoral thesis (Univ. de Barcelona).

——, 2002. 'La datación del *Cantar de Mio Cid* y el problema de su tradición manuscrita', in *Cid* 2002: 15–35.

——, & Ian MICHAEL , ed., 2008. *Cantar de Mio Cid* (Madrid: Castalia).

BLECUA, Alberto, 1983. *Manual de crítica textual*, Literatura y Sociedad, 33 (Madrid: Castalia).

BOWRA, C. M., 1952. *Heroic Poetry* (London: Macmillan).

CATALÁN, Diego, 2001. *La épica española: nueva documentación y nueva evaluación* (Madrid: Fundación Ramón Menéndez Pidal & Seminario Menéndez Pidal, 2000 [2001]).

CATANO, James V., 1988. *Language, History, Style: Leo Spitzer and the Critical Tradition* (Urbana: Univ. of Illinois Press; London: Routledge).

CHADWICK, H. Munro, & N. Kershaw CHADWICK, 1932–40. *The Growth of Literature*, 3 vols (Cambridge: UP).

Cid 1977. *'Mio Cid' Studies*, ed. A. D. Deyermond, CT, A59 (London: Tamesis Books).

——, 2002. *'Mio Cid' Studies: 'Some Problems of Diplomatic' Fifty Years On*, ed. Alan Deyermond, David G. Pattison, & Eric Southworth, PMHRS, 42.

CONDE, Juan-Carlos, 1999. 'Introducción', in Ramón MENÉNDEZ PIDAL & Juan-Carlos CONDE , 1999: 33–76.

DEYERMOND, Alan, 1969. *Epic Poetry and the Clergy: Studies on the 'Mocedades de Rodrigo'*, CT, A5 (London: Tamesis Books).

——, 1977. 'Tendencies in *Mio Cid* Scholarship, 1943–1973', in *Cid* 1977: 13–47.

——, 1982. 'The Close of the *Cantar de Mio Cid*: Epic Tradition and Individual Variation', in *The Medieval Alexander Legend and Romance Epic: Essays in Honour of David J. A. Ross*, ed. Peter Noble, Lucie Polak, & Claire Isoz (Millwood, NY: Kraus International), pp. 11–18.

———, 1992–93. 'Summing-Up', in 'Ramón Menéndez Pidal Twenty-Five Years On', ed. Alan Deyermond, *Journal of Hispanic Research*, 2, pp. 135–39.

———, 1995. *La literatura perdida de la Edad Media castellana: catálogo y estudio, I: épica y romances*, Obras de Referencia, 7 (Salamanca: Ediciones Universidad de Salamanca).

———, 1997. 'Sánchez's *Colección* and Percy's *Reliques*: The Editing of Medieval Poetry in the Dawn of Romanticism', in *Spain and its Literature: Essays in Memory of E. Allison Peers*, ed. Ann L. Mackenzie, Hispanic Studies TRAC, 15 (Liverpool: Liverpool UP & Modern Humanities Research Association), pp. 171–209.

———, & Margaret CHAPLIN, 1972. 'Folk-Motifs in the Medieval Spanish Epic', *Philological Quarterly*, 51: 36–53.

DUFFELL, Martin J., 2007. *Syllable and Accent: Studies on Medieval Hispanic Metrics*, PMHRS, 56.

DUGGAN, Joseph J., 1976. *A Guide to Studies on the 'Chanson de Roland'*, Research Bibliographies and Checklists, 15 (London: Grant & Cutler).

FLETCHER, Richard, 1989. *The Quest for El Cid* (London: Hutchinson).

FOGELQUIST, James Donald, ed., 2001. Pedro de Corral, *Crónica del rey don Rodrigo, postrimero rey de los godos (Crónica sarracina)*, CCa, 257–58 (Madrid: Castalia).

FOULET, Alfred, & Mary Blakely SPEER, 1979. *On Editing Old French Texts* (Lawrence: The Regents Press of Kansas).

FRADEJAS RUEDA, José Manuel, 1991. *Introducción a la edición de textos medievales castellanos*, Cuadernos de la UNED, 100 (Madrid: UNED).

FUNES, Leonardo, ed., 2007. Anónimo, *Poema de Mio Cid* (Buenos Aires: Colihue).

GOLDBERG, Harriet, in press. *Motif-Index of Medieval Hispanic Epic Legends*, Medieval & Renaissance Texts & Studies (Tempe, AZ: MRTS).

HATTO, A. T., 1989. 'Towards an Anatomy of Heroic and Epic Poetry', *Traditions of Heroic and Epic Poetry, II: Characteristics and Techniques*, ed. J. B. Hainsworth & A. T. Hatto, Publications of the MHRA, 13 (London: MHRA), pp. 145–306.

HERNÁNDEZ ALONSO, César, et al., ed., 1988. *'Poema de Mio Cid': edición facsímil del manuscrito del marqués de Pidal depositado en la Biblioteca Nacional*, 2 vols (Burgos: Ayuntamiento). Reprint of 1982 original.

HORRENT, Jules, ed. & tr., 1982. *Cantar de Mío Cid / Chanson de Mon Cid*, Ktëmata, 6, 2 vols (Gand: Éditions Scientifiques E. Story-Scientia).

HOUSMAN, A. E., 1961. *Selected Prose*, ed. John Carter (Cambridge: UP).

LACARRA LANZ, Eukene, 2005a. 'El linaje de Rodrigo Díaz', in *Story Weavers and Textual Critics Interpret the 'Poema de mio Cid'*, ed. Óscar Martín, C, 33.2, pp. 111–25.

———, 2005b. 'Sobre la historicidad de la leyenda de los Siete infantes de Lara', in *Historicist Essays on Hispano-Medieval Narrative in Memory of Roger*

M. Walker, ed. Barry Taylor & Geoffrey West, Publications of the MHRA, 16 (London: Maney Publishing for the MHRA), pp. 201–27.

——, 2007. 'Rodrigo Díaz re-visitado', in *Actas del XI Congreso Internacional de la Asociación Hispánica de Literatura Medieval (León, 20–24 de septiembre de 2005)*, ed. Armando López Castro & Luzdivina Cuesta Torre (León: Universidad), I, pp. 81–94.

LÓPEZ ESTRADA, Francisco, 1982. *Panorama crítico sobre el 'Poema del Cid'*, Literatura y Sociedad, 30 (Madrid: Castalia).

LORD, Albert B., 1960. *The Singer of Tales*, Harvard Studies in Comparative Literature, 24 (Cambridge, MA: Harvard UP).

MALKIEL, Yakov, 1969–70. 'Era omme esencial...', *RPh*, 23: 371–411.

MENÉNDEZ Y PELAYO, Marcelino, 1944–45. *Antología de poetas líricos castellanos*, ed. Enrique Sánchez Reyes, Edición Nacional de las Obras Completas de Menéndez Pelayo, 17–26 (Santander: CSIC).

Menéndez Pidal 1992–93. 'Ramón Menéndez Pidal Twenty-Five Years On', ed. Alan Deyermond, *Journal of Hispanic Research*, 2: 125–42.

MENÉNDEZ PIDAL, Ramón, 1899. 'Notas para el romancero del conde Fernán González', in *Homenaje a Menéndez y Pelayo en el año vigésimo de su profesorado: estudios de erudición española* (Madrid: Victoriano Suárez), I, pp. 429–507.

——, ed., 1908–11. *Cantar de Mio Cid: texto, gramática y vocabulario*, 3 vols (Madrid: Bailly-Baillière).

——, 1910. *L'Épopée castillane à travers la littérature espagnole* (Paris: Armand Colin).

——, ed., 1913. *Poema de Mio Cid*, Clásicos Castellanos, 24 (Madrid: La Lectura). Later impressions publ. by Espasa-Calpe.

——, 1922. *Poesía popular y poesía tradicional en la literatura española* (Oxford: Clarendon Press).

——, 1925. *El rey Rodrigo en la literatura* (Madrid: [RAE]).

——, 1934. *Historia y epopeya*, Obras de R. Menéndez Pidal, 2 (Madrid: Centro de Estudios Históricos).

——, 1945. *La epopeya castellana a través de la literatura española* (Buenos Aires: Espasa-Calpe Argentina).

——, ed., 1944–46. *'Cantar de Mio Cid': texto, gramática y vocabulario*, 2nd ed., Obras Completas de R. Menéndez Pidal, 3–5 (Madrid: Espasa-Calpe).

——, 1947. *La España del Cid*, 4th ed., 2 vols, Obras Completas de R. Menéndez Pidal, 6 & 7 (Madrid: Espasa-Calpe). First ed. 1929.

——, 1953. *Romancero hispánico (hispano-portugués, americano y sefardí): teoría e historia*, Obras Completas de R. Menéndez Pidal, 9–10 (Madrid: Espasa-Calpe).

——, 1956. 'Problemas de la épica española', in his *Los godos y la epopeya española: 'chansons de geste' y baladas nórdicas*, Colección Austral, 1275 (Madrid: Espasa-Calpe), pp. 59–87.

——, 1957. *Poesía juglaresca y orígenes de las literaturas románicas: problemas de historia literaria y cultural*, Biblioteca de Cuestiones Actuales, 6 (Madrid:

Instituto de Estudios Políticos). 2nd ed. of *Poesía juglaresca y juglares* (1924).

——, 1960. *La 'Chanson de Roland' et la tradition épique des Francs*, 2nd ed. [of Spanish original], tr. Irénée-Marcel Cluzel (Paris: A. et J. Picard).

——, 1961. 'Dos poetas en el *Cantar de Mio Cid'*, *Romania*, 82: 145–200.

——, 1964. 'Observaciones críticas sobre las biografías de Fray Bartolomé de las Casas', in *Actas del Primer Congreso Internacional de Hispanistas, celebrado en Oxford del 6 al 11 de septiembre de 1962*, ed. Frank Pierce & Cyril A. Jones (Oxford: Dolphin, for Asociación Internacional de Hispanistas), pp. 13–24.

——, 1971. *La leyenda de los infantes de Lara*, 3rd ed., ed. Diego Catalán, Obras Completas de R. Menéndez Pidal, 1 (Madrid: Espasa-Calpe).

——, 1992. *La épica medieval española desde sus orígenes hasta su disolución en el romancero*, ed. Diego Catalán & María del Mar de Bustos, Obras Completas de R. Menéndez Pidal, 13 (Madrid: Espasa-Calpe).

——, & Juan-Carlos CONDE, ed., tr. Alfonso REYES , 1999. *Cantar de Mio Cid*, prol. Martín de Riquer, Colección Austral, 20 (Madrid: Espasa-Calpe).

——, et al., ed., 1951. *Reliquias de la poesía épica española*, with Manuel Muñoz, José Gómez Pérez, Miguel Santiago, Diego Catalán Menéndez-Pidal, & Elvira Díaz Guardamino (Madrid: Instituto de Cultura Hispánica & CSIC).

——, et al., ed., 1980. *Reliquias de la poesía épica española, acompañadas de 'Epopeya y romancero'*, I, ed. Diego Catalán, Reliquias de la épica Hispánica, 1 (Madrid: Cátedra-Seminario Menéndez Pidal & Gredos). 2nd ed. of 1951.

MICHAEL, Ian, ed., 1978. *Poema de Mio Cid*, CCa, 75, 2nd ed. (Madrid: Castalia).

——, ed., tr. Rita HAMILTON & Janet PERRY, 1975. *The Poem of the Cid: A New Critical Edition of the Spanish Text* (Manchester: UP; New York: Barnes & Noble).

MILÁ Y FONTANALS, Manuel, 1959. *De la poesía heroico-popular castellana*, ed. Martín de Riquer & Joaquín Molas, Obras, I (Barcelona: CSIC). First publ. Barcelona: the author, 1874.

MILLET, Victor, 2007. *Héroes de libro: poesía heroica en las culturas anglogermánicas medievales* (Santiago de Compostela: Universidade).

MONTANER FRUTOS, Alberto, ed., 1993a. *Cantar de Mio Cid*, Biblioteca Clásica, 1 (Barcelona: Crítica).

——, 1993b. '*Cave carmen!*: de huellas de asonancia a "prosa rimada" en las prosificaciones épicas cronísticas', in *Actas do IV Congreso da Associação Hispânica de Literatura Medieval (Lisboa, Outubro 1–5 1991)*, ed. Aires A. Nascimento & Cristina Almeida Ribeiro, II, Medievalia, 7 (Lisboa: Edições Cosmos), pp. 67–72.

——, 1995. 'De nuevo sobre los versos iniciales perdidos del *Cantar de Mio Cid'*, en *Medioevo y literatura: Actas del V Congreso de la Asociación Hispánica*

de Literatura Medieval (Granada, 27 septiembre–1 octubre 1993), ed. Juan
Paredes (Granada: Univ. de Granada), III, pp. 341–60.
——, ed., 2007. *Cantar de Mio Cid*, Biblioteca Clásica (Barcelona: Centro
para la Edición de los Clásicos Españoles, Galaxia Gutenberg, & Círculo
de Lectores).
MOORMAN, Charles, 1975. *Editing the Middle English Manuscript* (Jackson:
UP of Mississippi).
ORDUNA, Germán, 1997. 'La edición crítica y el *codex unicus*: el texto
del *Poema de Mio Cid*', *Incipit*, 17: 1–46. Repr. in his *Fundamentos de
crítica textual*, ed. Leonardo Funes & José Manuel Lucía Megías (Madrid:
Arco/Libros, 2005), pp. 101–46.
PENNY, Ralph, 2002. 'Dialect Contact, Koineization, and the Language of
the *Poema de Mio Cid*', in *Cid* 2002: 91–102.
PÉREZ PASCUAL, José Ignacio, 1998. *Ramón Menéndez Pidal: ciencia y pasión*
(Valladolid: Consejería de Educación y Cultura, Junta de Castilla y León).
PÉREZ PRIEGO, Miguel Ángel, 1997. *La edición de textos*, Teoría de la Literatura
y Literatura Comparada, 20 (Madrid: Editorial Síntesis).
PÉREZ VILLANUEVA, Joaquín, 1991. *Ramón Menéndez Pidal: su vida y su tiempo*
(Madrid: Espasa-Calpe).
RUSSELL, P. E., 1952. 'Some Problems of Diplomatic in the *Cantar de Mio Cid*
and their Implications', *MLR*, 47: 340–49.
——, 2002. 'Reinventing an Epic Poet: 1952 in Context', in *Cid* 2002: 63–71.
SÁNCHEZ, Thomás Antonio, ed., 1779. *Colección de poesías castellanas anteriores
al siglo XV*, I: *Poema del Cid* (Madrid: Antonio de Sancha).
SANMATEU, Xelo, 1997. '*El Cid*, un ejemplo de épica cinematográfica: notas
sobre su uso del espectáculo', en *'Quien hubiese tal ventura': Medieval
Hispanic Studies in Honour of Alan Deyermond*, ed. Andrew M. Beresford
(London: Department of Hispanic Studies, Queen Mary and Westfield
College), pp. 23–34.
SMITH, Colin, ed., 1972. *Poema de Mio Cid* (Oxford: Clarendon Press).
——, ed., 1976. *Poema de Mio Cid*, Letras Hispánicas, 35 (Madrid: Cátedra).
2nd ed. 1985.
——, 1992. 'Dissonant Voices: Some Heterodox Spanish Views of the
Poema de mio Cid, 1911–68', *Anuario Medieval*, 4: 193–217.
WHITE, R. J., 1965. *Dr Bentley: A Study in Academic Scarlet* (London: Eyre &
Spottiswoode).

Vida latente, literatura viviente:
Menéndez Pidal and the *Romancero*, Forty Years On

GERALDINE COATES

(*St. Anne's College, University of Oxford*)

> *Upon those who step into the same rivers*
> *different and ever different waters flow down (Heraclitus)*

The debt of modern day medieval Hispanists to Ramón Menéndez Pidal is an irrefutable one, and the extent of this debt has been recognized by scholars past and present. Colin Smith, in his lecture of 1970 commemorating the centenary of the birth of Pidal, placed him at the very foundations of literary criticism, stating that no new work can be begun on the subjects of epic and ballad without a long period of study of Pidal's writings, and that hardly anything can be published without constant reference to him. Professor Alan Deyermond has in the past made an even firmer case for grounding medieval Hispanism in Pidalian endeavour, correctly observing that Pidal has provided much of the basic material on which we all work. This is very true of *Romancero* scholarship. Although collecting efforts for the *Romancero* now reach far and wide, and have depended on a host of individuals, they did in a sense begin with Pidal. In May 1900, while on honeymoon and during a solar eclipse, he and his wife happened upon a washerwoman in the Castilian town of Osma with a repository of traditional ballads, including a *romance noticiero* about the death of the Príncipe don Juan in 1497. It was proof of a living ballad tradition in Old Castile and the beginnings of its recovery, an event interpreted by Diego Catalán as 'el "alba" del romancero castellano' (1979b: 222), and by Pidal himself as 'el sol de la tradición castellana que [...] alboreaba tras una noche de tres siglos'.

These ballads had never disappeared, but had been existing latently, in darkness. This idea of latent life, *vida latente*, takes us to the heart of Pidal's thesis of traditionality, which is in itself central to our appreciation of his work on the *Romancero* and, in fact, a subject about which he spoke in the city of Oxford. In his lecture, 'Poesía popular y poesía tradicional' given in Oxford in the summer of 1922, Pidal explored the very essence of traditionality, suggesting that it was something more than popular reception or acceptance of poetry: implicit within it was the re-elaboration and renewal of existing forms through the means of variants. For Pidal, variation was the cornerstone of poetic life and its means of constant artistic renovation: 'Esta poesía que se rehace en cada repetición, que se refunde en cada una de sus variantes, las cuales viven y se propagan en ondas de carácter colectivo [...] es la poesía propiamente tradicional' (1922: 23). In fact, Pidal's own collection, the *Flor nueva de romances viejos*, first published in 1928, put variation at the heart of the public's experience of the Spanish ballad. This work was to provide a ballad anthology for popular consumption and Pidal states in the prefatory material that the reader will encounter variants on a single ballad, some of which are his 'propia inventiva' (39). In introducing variants, Pidal was making the point of following in the traditional ways of those who had elaborated the texts before him. His collection was, he posited, no less authentic for the intervention, rather more alive: 'vivir es variar' was his justification (39). If poetic life was variation, implicit in this was, however, loss of some kind. Some parts of this colourful whole were destined to be casualties of the latent life: simply forgotten, not necessarily for being of inferior quality, but for lacking the habitual *refundición* that was necessary to keep them alive. This was an idea that Pidal spoke of in his spirited defence of the *estado latente* at the age of ninety-four:

> Toda vida es producción de nuevas individualidades con muerte del ser que se reproduce, y la literatura colectiva es literatura viviente; vive en refundiciones, en variantes continuadas, destinadas a la muerte, vida latente en la mayor parte de su curso. (1963: 152)

If the threat of at least partial caducity looms, shadow-like, over oral tradition, then valuing the creativity of existing variants is essential to modern ballad studies. One of the aspects of traditionality that Pidal emphasized, inseparable from an artistic life of latency and variation, was that of the poetic creativity inherent in the oral tradition, and it is this particular aspect that I wish to pursue in more detail first.[1] His Oxford lecture set out a comparison of versions of the 'Conde Arnaldos' ballad, during which Pidal alluded to the 'fuerza innovadora' that lay behind variants (15).[2] He went on to assert, 'los variantes no son accidente inútil para el arte; son parte de la invención poética; la belleza más alta se puede revelar no sólo al primer cantor sino a cualquier recitador' (22). The oral aspect of the *Romancero* didn't attract significant critical attention, however, until the 1960s when several innovative studies dedicated to the creative aspect of the traditional ballads appeared, independently, by the authors Braulio do Nascimento (1964 and 1966), Giuseppe Di Stefano (1967), Joseph Szertics (1967) — who cites Pidal's work on tense usage in the *Cantar de Mio Cid* as one of the precendents for his study of tense forms in the *Romancero* (7) —, and Paul Bénichou in his groundbreaking monograph of 1968, *Creación poética en el romancero tradicional*. In the prologue to this work, Pidal's precedent is obvious, not just in Bénichou's reference to the *autor-legión*, but also in his allusions to the life of poetry as emanating from its creative diversity:

> El trabajo de la tradición merece ser estudiado como proceso creador, y la mejor forma de hacerlo es considerar un romance en la totalidad de sus versiones conocidas, antiguas y modernas [...] El autor-legión en sus tanteos, variantes y rehacimientos, hace lo mismo — fundamentalmente — que el poeta culto en sus correcciones y borradores [...] Aquí es donde se ve, mejor que en cualquier otra parte, nacer y vivir la poesía. (9)

Further studies during the 1970s and 1980s concentrated on this dynamic creative process. Articles by Diego Catalán (1970; 1970–71), John Cummins (1970), Mercedes Díaz Roig (1977), and Oro A. Librowicz (1981) stand out, as do papers by Catalán, Catalán & Catarella, and Suzanne H. Petersen in the final section of *El Romancero en la*

---

[1] Diego Catalán picks the *Flor nueva* out as representing a work 'en que el investigador del romancero y la épica abandona el terreno de la ciencia filológica para adentrarse, de mano del pueblo-autor, en el de la creación poética activa' (1979a: 108).

[2] I take into account Menéndez Pidal's distinction between version and variant: 'llamaré *versión* a la redacción completa o fragmentaria de un romance tomada en conjunto y en cuanto difiere de las demás redacciones totales del mismo; llamaré *variante* a cada uno de los pormenores de que se compone una versión, en cuanto ese pormenor difiere de los análogos contenidos en las demás versiones' (1973: 299).

tradición oral moderna (Catalán et al 1972) devoted to 'La creación poética en el Romancero oral moderno: Nuevos métodos de estudio', and by Joseph Silverman and Antonio Sánchez-Romeralo in the subsequent second volume of *El Romancero hoy* dedicated to *Poética* (Catalán et al 1979).

Whilst applauding Pidal's intuitive feeling for the creative poetics of the *Romancero*, Stephen Gilman, in his 1972 article on *Romancero* as a poetic language, challenged the way in which Pidal's theory of the relationship between epic and ballad had led to the production of a rhetorical category of 'epic-lyric' poetry, such as that which he identifies in *La epopeya castellana*: 'otras veces transporta el fragmento de estilo épico a un nuevo estilo épico-lírico' (1945: 139). Gilman took issue with the implicit assumption that the Romancero is a transitional poetry and by questioning Pidal's description of traditional style, and noting its failure to distinguish linguistic and stylistic phenomena and to take account of syntax, he argued that the *Romancero* must be understood on its own poetic terms; not as transitional but as a special and autonomous language, an 'organic unity [...] unique unto itself' (153–54).

By 1984, the Seminario Menéndez Pidal had produced the *Catálogo general del romancero*, preceded by a theoretical introduction by Diego Catalán and his collaborators. Herein, Catalán stressed vital points: the openness of the *romance* as a narrative structure, and its exposure to two governing forces: *herencia* and *innovación* (19). The creative product is interpreted here as illustrative of the real world, the social world in which it is produced; ballads are said always to project a simulation of the social reality in which they live. The introduction goes on to suggest that this openness creates ideological stances within ballads, always aspiring to reorganize and revise social reality and its values (21). The link between poetic creativity and society was continued in Catalán's article 'The Artisan Poetry of the *Romancero*' in the 1989 volume *Hispanic Balladry Today* edited by Ruth House Webber. In this later piece, he writes that 'the narration keeps on adapting itself, both aesthetically and ethically, to the changing systems of values of the social groups that make use of romances to express their most deep-seated, local, and intimate culture' (3).

Allied to this concern with the social context of ballad production is a critical desire to reassert the poetics of the *Romancero* and to provide tighter paradigmatic frameworks of analysis, often connected to the possibility of an underlying ideology. This is a feature of Ana Valenciano's article in the same *Hispanic Balladry* volume in which she states that 'the folkloric subject learns naturally the poetic discourse in which *romances* are expressed, and he makes use of them to set forth and to comment upon problems that interest or affect in some way the society in which he happened to be born' (28). From a sociolinguistic perspective, Louise Mirrer-Singer continued the theme of the open-endedness of the *Romancero* and developed critical discussions of structure and content, such as that of Webber (1951), by examining linguistic devices which support 'both the production and the reproduction of the romances' (1986: 6). Beatriz Mariscal Hay's article of 1992 continued to explore the poetics of traditional narrative poetry, again picking up Catalán's stress upon *apertura*, and the wider critical tradition of the creative oral process. Analyzing the function of stylistic resources of this creative process, she referred to the importance of cultural anxieties, and contemporary value systems (335), before concluding that ballad poetics rely as much on the ability to adhere to elements inherited from the past, as on a 'capacidad innovadora y creativa' (336). In an article of 1994, Teresa Catarella discussed what she called the past paradigms of study for the orally transmitted ballad, firmly identifying Pidal's evolutionary, dynamic model as one of them (472). In her exploration of the new parameters of oral poetics, she suggested that the nature and essence of the ballad, the phenomenon of transformation and variation, was a fundamental concern. She developed the idea that potentiality — 'not only what is said, in all its fluidity and variability, but what is unsaid' (475) — is the theoretical axis around which ballad poetics should revolve. It seems a fitting development of Pidal's *estado latente*, of a presence yet an absence at the same time.

Menéndez Pidal's ideas about variation, creation, latency, and the *autor-legión* are inherently connected to the issue of the geography of the *Romancero*, launched more specifically in 1920 in his study of the geographic diffusion of the ballads *Gerineldo* and *El conde sol*: 'Sobre geografía folklórica: Ensayo de un método', expanded and re-edited by Diego Catalán and Álvaro Galmés in 1954 (see Menéndez Pidal 1973). Pidal's work brought the transmission process to the heart of his definition of traditional poetry; it confirmed his theory of collective re-creation and the extent to which communal sensibilities and attitudes (artistic, moral, and ideological) inform, and even restrict, individual creative freedom. After meeting with criticism by Daniel Devoto in 1955, and with scepticism from Bénichou in 1968, Pidal's work in the area of folkloric geography was continued by Manuel Alvar in 1970 through his application of similar methods in the study of the widely diffused ballad 'Tamar y Amnón'.[3] It was further revindicated in the late 80s. Suzanne Petersen's defence of *Romancero* geography in an article of 1989 argued that the utility of geographic methods had been questioned and even played down in Hispanic ballad criticism to date (75). She reinstated the idea that ballad revisions were consistent with 'the prevailing attitudes and values of culturally bound collectivities' (78). Petersen's answer to past criticism of ballad geography was to adduce technical statistical evidence for the identification of evolutionary trends, thus making possible a more accurate characterization of the mechanisms of re-production and transformation of these oral narratives.[4] Her work was presented as objective proof of Pidal's argument that the ballad narrative of *La condesita* did not undergo parallel transformation throughout.[5]

Studies of the diffusion and geography of the ballad have attracted further critical interest up to the present day. The question of folkloric geography goes hand in hand with the practical collection of ballads through field work, an area of course in which Pidal's work was pathfinding as I pointed out earlier. Shortly after the discovery of the Old Castilian ballad tradition in 1900, around 1905, Pidal discovered that the oral ballad tradition was alive in South America and inspired generations of scholars to uncover the balladry of the New World. Catalán's efforts, with the aid of his international team, ensured that the work of Pidal in collecting ballads continued directly, and collecting enterprises have been sustained across the

---

[3] On Bénichou's divergence, see Petersen 1989: 84–85.

[4] She suggests that 'despite the difficulties inherent in the use of both space and time factors, these 2 variables are nonetheless essential to any theory which purports to define the processes of transformation and reproductive mechanisms of the romancero' (76).

[5] She found that the system opened up most in the last act of the ballad and that the singers of and within each region inevitably exercise the greatest creativity after they have received the better part of the ballad's actantial message (110).

world, from the Iberian Peninsula to Spanish America, Portugal, Brazil, Canada, Israel, North Africa, and the United States, to an extent that is difficult to rehearse sensibly here.[6]

In 1984, Samuel G. Armistead summarized the main areas of field work, stating that astounding results had been achieved in the early eighties, and naming Lusitanian balladry and Sephardic balladry as particularly strong fields of research. Reports of fieldwork since then can be found, for example, in Jesús Antonio Cid's 1994 article in *Ínsula*, and in the homage volume to Paul Bénichou, *La eterna agonía del romancero* (Piñero Ramírez 2001). Some outstanding titles have appeared which are testament to the continuing global reach of the collecting enterprise. Some of the most recent of these are, with reference to Spain, Petersen's *Romances de Zamora y Salamanca* (2004), Pedro Piñero Ramírez's *Romancero de la provincia de Huelva* (also 2004), the *Romancero de la provincia de Cádiz*, edited by Virtudes Atero Burgos (1996), and Michèle S. de Cruz Sáenz's *Traditional Ballads of Aragon* (1995). Outside of Spain, recent titles include Mercedes Díaz Roig's *Romancero tradicional de América* (1990), Beatriz Mariscal's *Romancero general de Cuba* (1996), Gloria Chicote's *Romancero tradicional Argentino* (2002), and Cruz-Sáenz's *Romancero tradicional de Costa Rica* (1986) and more recent article on ballads from Rocha, Uruguay (2005). Worthy of mention too are Maximiano Trapero's *Romancero tradicional canario* (1989), and his more recent publication derived from the conference *Romancero de la Gomera y el romancero general a comienzos del tercer milenio* (2003). As for Lusitanian balladry, Manuel Da Costa Fontes stands out as having ensured a productive line of research to more recent times, with a very recent article on *La condesa traidora* in the Portuguese oral tradition (2006). Following a round table discussion of the actual state of research on the modern ballad tradition at the 1999 'Encuentro internacional sobre el romancero', Enrique Baltanás reasserted the importance of Pidal in guiding research into the textual corpus of the modern tradition, and stated that 'el romancero de la tradición moderna es obra de Menéndez Pidal' (Piñero Ramírez 2001: 290).

The modern field of research into Sephardic ballad diffusion merits special attention, due to the truly impressive work of Armistead

---

[6]On the collecting efforts of the Seminario, see Petersen et al. 1982.

and Joseph Silverman, with the collaboration of Israel J. Katz as musicologist. Don Ramón was drawn to this branch of the *Romancero* and his interest in Judeo-Spanish culture lasted throughout his life. In 1906, and after correspondence with several Jewish scholars, he produced the 'Catálogo del romancero judío-español', which included 143 ballads. Deyermond has called the early date at which he realized the importance of the Sephardic tradition 'remarkable' (1993–94: 137). In 1976, Armistead produced *El romancero judeo-español en el archivo Menéndez Pidal*, a study of the ballads and songs collected by Pidal supported by articles underlining its importance for ballad research, and in 1977 edited with Silverman, *Romanceros judeo-españoles de Tánger*. For several decades, Armistead and Silverman have been guiding and stimulating research on the Judeo-Spanish tradition. The series *Folk-Literature of the Sephardic Jews* has been a monumental contribution, comprising volumes on Judeo-Spanish chapbooks, epic ballads, and Carolingian ballads (1971, 1986, 1994). The work *En torno al romancero sefardí (hispanismo y balcanismo de la tradición judeo-española)*, dating from 1982, revised and united several important studies. In the article 'The Judeo-Spanish Ballad Tradition' in *Hispanic Balladry Today* from 1989, Armistead and Silverman stress the crucial role of the Judeo-Spanish tradition in the diverse research orientations then being developed by Hispanism, which they list as: 'historical and source work, comparative studies [...], ballad geography, music, bibliography and cataloguing, literary criticism, oral creativity, sociological perspectives, formulism, semiotics, and computerized investigations' (244). They do, however, also acknowledge that time is running out for a tradition clearly in the final stages of decline; its latent life may be coming to an end. Much of it now lives electronically however; an online multimedia archive of ballads and other oral literature in Judeo-Spanish collected from 1957 to 1993 is available courtesy of Armistead, the late Joseph H. Silverman, and Israel J. Katz.

The movement from ballad geography to ballad ideology is a logical progression of Pidal's work which has seen critical interest in recent times. In 1972, Smith wrote of the 'ethos' of the *Romancero viejo*, suggesting that it must have something collectively to say, a set of basic attitudes. He quoted Pidal's prior statements to this effect, both of which are worth repeating: 'El romancero, en fin, por su tradicionalismo, por la cantidad de vida histórica que representa y por la multitud de reflejos estéticos y morales, es quintaesencia de características españolas' (1976: 40); 'El romancero recoge el espíritu de la epopeya, que desde los siglos más remotos, desde los primeros albores de la producción intelectual de la nación, informaba un sentir, un pensar común' (1953, I, xix).   The article develops the introduction to the original 1964 edition of *Spanish Ballads*, in which Smith discussed themes and sentiments, suggesting the importance of two above all: justice (which highlights the ballads' bias for vassal over king), and the tragic sense of life.   Of importance to later criticism, Smith argues that the ballads are not directly patriotic, nor do they concern themselves directly with the spirit and activities of the Reconquest (8). He posits too that the ballads are not 'anti-establishment' songs of protest, although their attitudes towards royalty and churchmen reveal distance from 'official attitudes of respect' (15) and a 'healthy detachment' (24).

In 1979, Julio Rodríguez Puértolas examined the relationship between man and his surroundings in the *Romancero*, his attempts at communication with the outside world which so frequently reveal his isolation and conflict. He concluded that 'El romancero es la historia de una frustración. La del ser humano en un momento de crisis religiosa, política y social, histórica. La del hombre moderno' (104). Antonio Lorenzo Vélez resumed the question of the ballads' ideology and vision of the world in the *Actas del IV Coloquio Internacional del Romancero* (published 1989), positing that the sociocultural context of the *Romancero* had been scarcely treated up to that point. He questioned the ballads' supposedly combative relationship with the cultural hegemony and dominant class, arguing against a unicity of vision and sustaining that the frame of reference of the *Romancero* is a wide and complex amalgamation of interests and postures which demands certain refining before ideological readings can take place.[7] Giuseppe Di Stefano takes up the *frustración* of the ballads in his article of 2000, linking it to the desiring gaze of the king, and the more general theme of 'la aspereza o más bien la impotencia del poder, cuando no su propia caída irremediable' (136).

Recent work in an ideological vein, and linked to authority and

---

[7] E. M. Wilson had concluded in 1958 that the ballads were 'class-conscious [...] but not conscious of class war' (1958: 22), showing an early precedent to these ideas.

power, has addressed the *fronterizo* ballads. We might cite the articles of Angus Mackay on aspects of frontier life (1976, 1989), in the more recent of which he suggests that the frontier ballads 'demonstrate a striking ability to see matters from the other's point of view' (225), a view advanced as early as the nineteenth century by Milá y Fontanals (1874). This Islamophile leaning was demonstrated by Pidal himself and has been supported by Smith (1972: 8–9, 18–19); Deyermond (1973: 227), David William Foster (1973–74), and L. P. Harvey (1990: 222 & 253) among others. Louise Mirrer-Singer has carefully explored the inscription of ideology in the composition and reception of frontier ballads and identifies Christian ideological motivation to ballads like 'Álora' and 'La morilla burlada' (1984–85, 1996: 25–30), and 'Jugando estaba el rey moro' (1994). That these ballads might serve a Christian cause has also been explored by Roger Wright (1987: 232 & 1991: 51), Barry Jackson (1990–91), Deyermond (1992: 97–109 & 1996: 32–35), and Jan Gilbert, with particular reference to postcolonial theory (2003). Most recently, Michael Gerli has studied the religious and cultural connotations of 'Álora' through an allusive discourse of biblical and textual genealogies (2005).

With ideological discussion comes consideration of gender and culture, another flourishing modern-day critical field. This was an issue Catalán picked up in his preface to the *Catálogo general* of 1984:

> Dado el papel preponderante que en la transmisión del romancero viene teniendo la mujer desde hace siglos [...] los romances que actualmente se cantan o recitan representan, sin duda, un enjuiciamiento del mundo referencial que ha de considerarse en buena parte como expresión de una perspectiva femenina. (21)

Pidal himself was obviously aware of the female role in the transmission and reinvigoration of traditional romances; in the 'proemio' to the *Flor nueva* he alludes to the ballads he heard during his childhood, 'los romances [...] reanimados por frescas voces femeninas, contagiadas de la afición' (1976: 41). However, the female role, which Pidal seems to have taken as understood, is an aspect of the recreation of tradition that has been of more specific interest in recent times. That is not to underplay Pidalian precedent. Pidal's insistence upon the open and creative aspect of oral tradition is, for example, central to the work of Beatriz Mariscal de Rhett who confirms from experience in collecting ballads that 'the majority of informants, and therefore the principal depositaries of oral traditions, are women', adding that the active role of women in the creative process, the incorporation of their voices and their world views, has necessarily been a determining factor in their function and structure (1989: 257–58).[8]

Smith points out in his 1996 prologue to *Spanish Ballads* that themes and sentiments in the living *Romancero* must respond in some measure to women's concerns and feelings, citing Teresa Catarella's article on feminine historicizing, in which she identifies in the *Romancero* an implicit subversion of traditional male authority, as a productive start. Acknowledging the excellence of Catarella's article, Wright nevertheless reminds us of the powerful appeal of universal human emotions, 'most of the emotions felt by protagonists within the ballads can be experience by anyone in the audience, of whatever gender' (2004: 173). Ian Michael seemed to suggest a dead end in stating in 1996 that 'the collectors give us so appallingly little information that we cannot analyze the position further, except to note the enormous preponderance of women' (100–01). He did, however, use the framework of gender to gesture towards a lack of direct connection between ballad and epic, based on a divergence in ethos:

> women characters in the ballad often exhibit a freedom of action and express a bold, self-willed sexuality rarely to be found in more male-oriented and male-composed texts, such as the epic [...] Thematically the epic offers us a man's world of military and diplomatic action, conjured up by male poets and male singers [...] The ballad constituted the one vehicle in which ordinary women could express their emotions and ambitions, and was traditionally passed down and recreated by them. (101)[9]

---

[8]Frank Odd would suggest that 'the collective, popular imagination which shaped the ballads projected a vision of women as a stabilizing and humanizing force with the feudal world of male ambition' (1983: 368).

[9]Recent criticism has provided readings of female ballad characters which supports this view. See, for example, González Troyano 1989, Mirrer-Singer 1995, Vasvári 1999, Suárez Robaina 2003.

Lucy Sponsler's work on Women in the *Medieval Spanish Epic and Lyric Traditions* (1975) seems to approach the issue from entirely the opposite position, relying heavily, as Richard Kinkade's review points out, 'on the earlier works of Menéndez Pidal whose neotraditionalist theories of the epic cycle from inception, to prosification in the chronicles, to fragmentation and dispersion in ballad form, provide the framework for the development of feminine characterization' (1976: 953).

I have gone this far without fully delving into what Pidal regarded as a close and traditional relationship between ballad and epic: 'Todas las gestas se hicieron romances; es que la epopeya se hizo romancero' (1953, I: 193). In the 1996 prologue to his *Spanish Ballads*, Smith states that in the first edition of the book in 1964 'it seemed natural enough to adopt almost unquestioningly the "traditionalist" (later "neotraditionalist") theory of epic and ballad origins developed and perfected by Ramón Menéndez Pidal' (xii). His revised assessment was that 'since 1964 research and weight of argument have greatly altered ideas about how medieval epic was created in France and Spain (and the dependence of the latter on the former in some regards), while Menéndez Pidal's views of the ballad genre have remained substantially unaffected' (xii). It is reasonable to suggest that many of Pidal's ideas about the origins of ballads in epic can be allowed to stand, although necessary to revisit briefly the debate between traditionalist and individualist schools which challenged these ideas in very productive ways.

In the late seventies and early eighties (1978, 1981) Armistead voiced reservations about a critical trend which appeared to be supplanting Pidal's traditionalist theories of the medieval Spanish epic, a so-called neo-individualist theory expounded by the likes of Peter Russell, Deyermond, in his monograph on *Epic Poetry and the Clergy*, Smith, and Cummins. Asserting that the *Romancero*'s connection with the epic was 'complex and diversified — a variety of contacts, among which fragmentation was only one possible modality', Armistead rejected neo-individualism as a complete, alternative hypothesis to Pidal's (1981: 384). In 1986, in a challenging article in *La Corónica*, Wright suggested that ballads may be much older than had hitherto been believed, and may have preceded respective epic texts, a view which prompted a quick response from Armistead.

Despite admitting that the ballad genre may be a very old one, Armistead rejected the notion that Spanish epics were made up of a series of autonomous ballads, and affirmed that the *cantares* could refer to longer, epic poems rather than the shorter source poems Wright had proposed (1986–87: 53–54). Wright responded by clarifying the terms of the debate and exploring the possibility that the likely existence of the ballad genre in the twelfth century could explain some of the characteristics of the epic *Poema de Mio Cid* (1989–90). In 1992, Armistead again underlined his support of traditionalist theories, stating that investigations into epic poetry outside the Peninsula offered theoretical models similar to those set out by Pidal (4). His conclusion, preceded by the suggestion that neoindividualist criticism has offered scepticism but not alternatives, reads firmly in defence of Pidal:

> Dada la esencial fluidez de la poesía oral, la multiplicidad de versiones variantes, la flexibilidad de las 'fronteras' entre los diversos relatos tradicionales y las demás circunstancias y testimonios internacionales [...] la idea pidalina de que los romances surgieron como fragmentos o resúmenes de los cantares de gesta se nos ofrece ahora como eminentemente razonable y convincente. (14)

Deyermond, summing up the 1993 Queen Mary Medieval Hispanic Research Seminar dedicated to the then standing of the work of Pidal suggested that 'although Menéndez Pidal's work on the epic can now be seen to have major weaknesses as well as major strengths, his ballad research stands secure. With few exceptions, what is needed is not revision but continuation' (1993–94: 137).[10] In 2005, Irene Zaderenko did just that, providing a fresh challenge to Pidal's epic-derivative theory by suggesting that few *romances viejos* directly reflect scenes from the *Poema de Mio Cid*, only three developing episodes from the poem: 'Helo, helo, por do viene', 'Por Guadalquivir arriba' and 'Tres cortes'. Her view is that the *romances viejos* which recreate scenes from the *Poema* fit and broaden Pidal's very restricted category of romances 'de libre invención' and reveal poetic and thematic traits from the *Romancero* of the fifteenth and sixteenth centuries.

---

[10]The long history of British admiration for Menéndez Pidal, despite various challenges to his views, is also emphasized there and is worthy of re-emphasis in the context of *Romancero* studies.

So what of the future directions of ballad research post-Pidal? In 2003, Armistead wrote that outstanding collecting efforts are still going forward on many fronts, but these efforts have 'coincided with an intense awareness of the progressive disappearance of many forms of oral tradition' (155). In 2001, Jesús-Antonio Cid stated that interest ought also to be taken in the motivations of those collecting 'para saber por qué tenemos el romancero que tenemos y no otro' (286). Closely connected with the collecting enterprise and its ethos is that of cataloguing, classifying, computerizing and organizing ballad material. In 1967, Don Ramón left to Diego Catalán 'la totalidad de los restantes trabajos en preparación y estudio, sobre los que viene trabajando en el Archivo Menéndez Pidal, con la recomendación de que ponga todo su interés y voluntad en continuarlos, para que puedan ser publicados' (cited in Armistead 2000: 457). With this legacy came the need to create a classifying system to make these research materials readily available which took important steps forward in the heroic *Catálogo General del Romancero* (CGR), and in the publication in 1998 of two volumes of the *Catálogo analítico del Archivo Romancístico Menéndez Pidal-Goyri*. The online Pan-Hispanic ballad project, led by Petersen, is a more recently developed classifying resource, combining several interrelated databases that provide students in this field with essential tools for their research comprising bibliography, cartography, ballad texts, as well as digitized reproductions of original oral performances and their musical notation. In 2005, Petersen paid homage to Harriet Goldberg's monumental project on folk motifs involving the *Romancero* which has since been incorporated into the website. The future also seems to hold more steps towards collaborative work, as noted by Armistead (1984), Catarella (1994), Cid (2001), and Petersen (2003).[11] Collection and organization of material must also be accompanied by interpretation; as Ian Michael puts it, the interest of the ballad scholar should be to 'study its interaction and intercutting with learned literature over the centuries, and to analyse and admire the great aesthetic effects of which it is capable' (1996: 102). Wright, following his emphasis on the role of the ballad performer (2000), has also spoken out in

---

[11]She suggests that the pan-Hispanic Romancero merits attention 'for its complex interconnections both with other Hispanic and pan-European verbal art forms and with the learned literary and musical traditions of the Peninsula and beyond' (169).

favour of listening and watching modern performances in order to gain a better and fuller idea of what the older oral genre was like than simply relying on sixteenth-century written texts (2004: 180).

Over forty years after his death, Ramón Menéndez Pidal's work in the field of *Romancero* studies is standing up remarkably well to the test of time. In the sense that his research continues to furnish scholars with inroads into a closer and more informed appreciation of the *Romancero,* his work remains open-ended, like the ballad material in hand. Pidal once prided himself on being the Spaniard who had heard and read the most *romances* (1976: 41) and so close was he to the tradition that it seems to carry something of him within it. Paul Bénichou reflects that within the *Romancero* death and life are close partners, 'dentro del Romancero, lo muerto y lo vivo conviven [...] la obra total, antigua y moderna, del poeta legión hispánico ha merecido y conseguirá la inmortalidad' (1989: 745). To this we might add that in this living literature lie the traces of a life's work, often *latentes,* but not to be forgotten.

Works Cited

ALVAR, Manuel, 1970. *El Romancero: tradicionalidad y pervivencia* (Barcelona: Planeta).

ARMISTEAD, Samuel G., 1976. *El romancero judeo-español en el archivo Menéndez Pidal* (Catálogo-índice de romances y canciones) (Madrid: Gredos).

——, 1978. 'The *Mocedades de Rodrigo* and Neo-Individualist Theory', *HR*, 46: 313–27.

——, 1981. 'Epic and Ballad: A Traditionalist Perspective', *Olifant*, 8: 376–88.

——, 1984. 'Current Trends in *Romancero* Research', *C*, 13: 23–36.

——, 1986–87. '*Encore les cantilenes!* Prof. Roger Wright's Proto-Romances', *C*, 15: 52–66.

——, 1992. 'Los orígenes épicos del romancero en una perspective multicultural', in *Estudios de folklore y literatura dedicados a Mercedes Díaz Roig*, ed. Beatriz Garza Cuarón & Yvette Jiménez de Báez, Estudios de Lingüística y Literatura, 20 (México: Colegio de México), pp. 1–15.

——, 2000. 'Review: *Catálogo Analítico del Archivo Romancístico Menéndez Pidal-Goyri, A: Romances de tema nacional*', *HR*, 68: 457–59.

——, 2003. 'Pan-Hispanic Oral Tradition', *Oral Tradition*, 18: 154–56.

ARMISTEAD, Samuel G. & Joseph SILVERMAN, 1971. *The Judeo-Spanish Chapbooks of Yacob Abraham Yoná*, Folk Literature of the Sephardic Jews, 1 (Berkeley: University of California Press).

——, 1977. *Romanceros judeo-españoles de Tánger* (Madrid: Gredos).

——, 1982. *En torno al romancero sefardí (hispanismo y balcanismo de la tradición judeo-española)*, Fuentes para el estudio del romancero. Serie Sefardí, 7 (Madrid: Seminario Menéndez Pidal, Universidad Complutense de Madrid).

——, 1986. *Judeo-Spanish Ballads from Oral Tradition: I, Epic Ballads*, Folk Literature of the Sephardic Jews, 2 (Berkeley: University of California Press).

——, 1989. 'The Judeo-Spanish Ballad Tradition', in Webber 1989: 235–46.

——, 1994. *Judeo-Spanish Ballads from Oral Tradition: II, Carolingian Ballads, 1 Roncesvalles*, Folk Literature of the Sephardic Jews, 3 (Berkeley: University of California Press).

ATERO BURGOS, Virtudes et al., ed., 1996. *Romancero de la provincia de Cádiz*, Romancero general de Andalucía, 1 (Cádiz: Universidad, 1996).

BÉNICHOU, Paul, 1968. *Creación poética en el romancero tradicional*, Biblioteca Románica Hispánica: Estudios y ensayos, 2 (Madrid: Gredos).

CATALÁN, Diego, 1970. *Por campos del romancero: Estudios sobre la tradición oral moderna* (Madrid).

——, 1970–71. 'Memoria e invención en el Romancero de tradición oral', *RPh*, 4: 1–25, 441–63.

——, 1972. 'La creación tradicional en la crítica reciente', in his *El romancero en la tradición oral moderna*, pp. 153–65.

——, & Teresa CATARELLA. 1972. 'El romancero tradicional, un sistema abierto', in *El romancero en la tradición oral moderna*, ed. Diego Catalán et al (Madrid: Cátedra-Seminario Menéndez Pidal y Rectorado de la Universidad de Madrid), pp. 181–205.

——, 1979a. 'El modelo de investigación pidalino cara al mañana' in *¡Alça la voz, pregonero! Homenaje a Don Ramón Menéndez Pidal, organizado por la Corporación de antiguos alumnos de la Institución Libre de Enseñanza* (Madrid: Cátedra-Seminario Menéndez Pidal), pp. 81–124.

——, 1979b. 'El romancero de tradición oral en el último cuarto del siglo XX', in his *El Romancero hoy*, I, pp. 219–56.

——, ed., 1982–84. *Catálogo general del romancero*, 3 vols (Madrid: Seminario Menéndez Pidal).

——, 1989. 'The Artisan Poetry of the *Romancero*', in Webber 1989: 1–25.

CATALÁN, Diego, Samuel G. ARMISTEAD & Antonio SÁNCHEZ-ROMERALO, eds., 1972. *El romancero en la tradición oral moderna: 1er Coloquio Internacional*, Romancero y poesía oral, 1 (Madrid: Cátedra-Seminario Menéndez Pidal y Rectorado de la Universidad de Madrid).

CATALÁN, Diego, Antonio SÁNCHEZ-ROMERALO, Samuel G. ARMISTEAD, Jesús Antonio CID, eds., 1979. *El Romancero hoy: 2º Coloquio Internacional*, University of California, Davis; Cátedra Seminario Menéndez Pidal; Universidad Complutense de Madrid; CILAS, University of California, San Diego, Romancero y poesía oral, 2–4, 3 vols (Madrid : Gredos).

CATARELLA, Teresa, 1990. 'Feminine Historicizing in the *Romancero novelesco*', *BHS*, 67: 331–43.

——, 1994. 'The Study of the Orally Transmitted Ballad: Past Paradigms and a New Poetics', *Oral Tradition*, 9: 468–78.

CHICOTE, Gloria B., 2002. *Romancero tradicional Argentino*, PMHRS, 25 (London: Department of Hispanic Studies, Queen Mary & Westfield College).

CID, Jesús-Antonio, 1994. 'El romancero tradicional hispánico. Obra infinida y campo abierto', *Ínsula*: 2–7.

CRUZ SÁENZ, Michèle S. de, 1986. *Romancero tradicional de Costa Rica*, Juan de la Cuesta Hispanic Monographs, Ediciones críticas, 3 (Newark, Delaware: Juan de la Cuesta).

——, 1995. *Spanish Traditional Ballads of Aragon* (Lewisburg: Bucknell University Press; London: Associated University Presses).

——, 2005. 'Romances de Rocha, Uruguay', in *'Entra mayo y sale abril': Medieval Spanish Literary and Folklore Studies in Memory of Harriet Goldberg*, ed. Manuel Da Costa Fontes & Joseph T. Snow, Juan de la Cuesta Hispanic Monographs, Homenajes, 25 (Newark, Delaware: Juan de la Cuesta), pp. 57–113.

CUMMINS, John B., 1970. 'The Creative Process in the Ballad "Pártese el moro Alicante"', *Forum for Modern Language Studies*, 6: 368–81.

DEVOTO, Daniel, 1955. 'Sobre el estudio folklórico del romancero español,

Proposiciones para un método de estudio de transmisión tradicional', *BH*, 57: 233–91.

DEYERMOND, Alan, 1969. *Epic Poetry and the Clergy: Studies on the 'Mocedades de Rodrigo'*, CT, A5 (London: Tamesis Books).

——, 1973. *Historia de la literatura española, I: La Edad Media*, Letras e Ideas: Instrumenta, 1 (Barcelona: Ariel).

——, 1992. '"Álora la bien cercada": Structure, Image, and Point of View in a Frontier Ballad', in *Hispanic Medieval Studies in Honor of Samuel G. Armistead*, ed. E. Michael Gerli & Harvey L. Sharrer (Madison: HSMS), pp. 97–109.

——, 1993–94. 'Summing Up', in 'The Work of Menéndez Pidal Twenty-Five Years On', *Journal of Hispanic Research*, 2: 135–39.

——, 1996. *Point of View in the Ballad: 'The Prisoner', 'The Lady and the Shepherd', and Others*, The Kate Elder Lecture, 7 (London: Dept of Hispanic Studies, Queen Mary and Westfield College).

DI STEFANO, G., 1967. *Sincronia e diacronia nel Romanzero* (Pisa: Università di Pisa), pp. 127–37.

——, 2000. 'El rey que mira. Poder y poesía en el romancero viejo', in *Historia, reescritura y pervivencia del romancero: Estudios en memoria de Amelia García-Valdecasas*, ed. Luis Beltrán (València: Universitat), pp. 127–37.

DÍAZ-ROIG, Mercedes, 1977. 'Palabra y contexto en la recreación del Romancero tradicional', *NRFH*, 26: 460–67.

——, 1990. *Romancero tradicional de América* (México: Colegio de México).

DO NASCIMENTO, Braulio, 1964, 1966. 'Processos de variação do romance', *Revista Brasileira de Folclore*, 4: 59–125 & 6: 159–90.

FONTES, Manuel da Costa, 2006. 'Between Ballad and Parallelistic Song: *A condessa traidora* in the Portuguese Oral Tradition', in *Medieval and Renaissance Spain and Portugal: Studies in Honor of Arthur L-F. Askins*, ed. Martha E. Schaffer & Antonio Cortijo Ocaña (Woodbridge, Suffolk: Tamesis), pp. 182–98.

FOSTER, David William, 1973. 'A Note on the Rhetorical Structure of the Ballad *Álora la bien cercada*', *Romance Notes*, 15: 392–396.

GERLI, Michael, 2005. '"Call me Ishmael": Onomastics, Genealogies, and Ideologies in a Frontier Ballad (*Álora la bien cercada*)', in *'Entra mayo y sale abril': Medieval Spanish Literary and Folklore Studies in Memory of Harriet Goldberg*, ed. Manuel Da Costa Fontes & Joseph T. Snow, Juan de la Cuesta Hispanic Monographs, Homenajes, 25 (Newark, Delaware: Juan de la Cuesta), pp. 161–79.

GILBERT, Jan, 2003. '*Álora, Abenámar*, and Orientalism', *Proceedings of the Twelfth Colloquium*, ed. Alan Deyermond & Jane Whetnall, PMHRS, 35 (London: Department of Hispanic Studies, Queen Mary, University of London), pp. 49–61.

GILMAN, S., 1972. 'On Romancero as a Poetic Language', in *Crítica y poesía: Homenaje a Casalduero*, (Madrid: Gredos), pp. 151–60.

GONZÁLEZ TROYANO, Alberto, 1989. 'Algunos rasgos del arquetipo de la mujer seductora en el romancero tradicional andaluz', in *El romancero. Tradición y pervivencia a fines del siglo XX: Actas del IV Coloquio Internacional del Romancero* (Sevilla-Puerto de Santa María-Cádiz, 23–26 Junio de 1987), ed. Pedro Piñero Ramírez et al (Cádiz: Fundación Machado), pp. 549–51.

HARVEY, L. P. 1990. *Islamic Spain 1250–1500* (Chicago: Univ. of Chicago Press).

JACKSON, Barry B., 1990–91. 'Racial Prejudice and the Frontier Ballads', *Revista de Estudios Hispánicos* (Puerto Rico), pp. 17–18: 29–36.

KINKADE, Richard, 1976. Review of Sponsler, Lucy A. *Women in the Medieval Spanish Epic and Lyric Traditions, Hispania*, 59: 953–54.

LIBROWICZ, Oro A., 1981. 'Creación poética en tres versiones sefardíes del romance de Espinelo', *C*, 10: 59–64.

LORENZO VÉLEZ, Antonio, 1989. 'Ideología y visión del mundo en el romancero tradicional', in *El romancero. Tradición y pervivencia a fines del siglo XX: Actas del IV Coloquio Internacional del Romancero* (Sevilla-Puerto de Santa María-Cádiz, 23–26 Junio de 1987), ed. Pedro Piñero Ramírez et al (Cádiz: Fundación Machado), pp. 93–100.

MACKAY, Angus, 1976. 'The Ballad and the Frontier in Late Medieval Spain', *BHS*, 53: 15–33.

——, 1989. 'Religion, Culture, and Ideology on the Late Medieval Castilian-Granadan Frontier', in *Medieval Frontier Societies*, ed. Robert Bartlett & Angus MacKay (Oxford: Clarendon), pp. 217–43.

MARISCAL HAY, Beatriz, 1992. 'En busca de El caballo robado: hacia una poética de la poesía narrativa tradicional', in *Estudios de folklore y literatura dedicados a Mercedes Díaz Roig*, ed. Beatriz Garza Cuarón & Yvette Jiménez de Báez, Estudios de Lingüística y Literatura, 20 (México: Colegio de México), pp. 325–37.

——, 1996. *Romancero general de Cuba*, Estudios de lingüística y literatura, 31 (México: Colegio de México, Centro de Estudios Lingüísticos y Literarios).

MARISCAL DE RHETT, Beatriz, 1989. 'Structure and Functions of Oral Tradition', in Webber 1989: 247–68.

MENÉNDEZ PIDAL, Ramón, 1922. *Poesía popular y poesía tradicional en la literatura española* (Oxford: Imprenta Clarendoniana).

——, 1945. *La epopeya castellana a través de la literatura española* (Madrid: Espasa-Calpe).

——, 1953. *Romancero hispánico, hispano-portugués, americano y sefardí: teoría y historia*, 2 vols (Madrid: Espasa-Calpe).

——, 1963. 'El estado latente en la vida tradicional', *Revista de Occidente*, pp. 129–52.

——, 1973. *Estudios sobre el romancero, Obras completas* (Madrid: Espasa-Calpe), XI.

——, 1976. *Flor nueva de romances viejos* (Madrid: Espasa Calpe), first published 1928.

MICHAEL, Ian, 1996. 'Factitious Flowers or Fictitious Fossils: The *romances viejos* Re-viewed', in *Al que en buen hora nascio: Essays...in Honour of Colin Smith* (Liverpool: UP), pp. 91–105.

MILÁ Y FONTANALS, Manuel, 1959. *De la poesía heróico-popular castellana*, 2nd edn (first published 1874), ed. Martín de Riquer & Joaquín Molas, Obras, 1 (Barcelona: CSIC).

MIRRER-SINGER, Louise, 1984–85. 'Reevaluating the *Fronterizo* Ballad: The *Romance de la morilla burlada* as a Pro-Christian Text', *C*, 13: 157–67.

——, 1986. *The Language of Evaluation: A Sociolinguistic Approach to the Story of Pedro el Cruel in Ballad and Chronicle*, Purdue University Monographs in Romance Languages, 20 (Philadelphia: John Benjamins).

——, 1994. 'Representing "Other" Men: Muslims, Jews, and Masculine Ideals in Medieval Castilian Epic and Ballad', in *Medieval Masculinities: Regarding Men in the Middle Ages*, ed. Clare A. Lees (Minneapolis: Univ. of Minnesota Press), pp. 169–186.

——, 1995. 'Men's Language, Women's Power: Female Voices in the Romancero Viejo' in *Oral Tradition and Hispanic Literature: Essays in Honor of Samuel G. Armistead*, ed. Mishael M. Caspi, Manuel da Costa Fontes, & Israel J. Katz (New York: Garland), pp. 522–47.

——, 1996. *Women, Jews, and Muslims in the Texts of Reconquest Castile* (Ann Arbor: Univ. of Michigan Press).

ODD, Frank, 1983. 'Women of the Romancero: A Voice of Reconciliation', *Hispania*, 66: 360–68.

PETERSEN, Suzanne A., 1972. 'Cambios estructurales en el romancero tradicional', in *El romancero en la tradición oral moderna*, ed. Diego Catalán et al (Madrid: Cátedra-Seminario Menéndez Pidal y Rectorado de la Universidad de Madrid), pp. 167–79.

——, 1989. 'In Defence of Romancero Geography', in Webber 1989: 74–116.

PETERSEN, Suzanne H., et al, ed., 1982. *Voces nuevas del romancero castellano-leonés*, 2 vols (Madrid: Gredos).

——, 2003. 'Towards Greater Collaboration in Oral Tradition Studies', *Oral Tradition*, 18: 169–71.

——, 2004. *Romances de Zamora y Salamanca (2001–2002)* (Madrid: Instituto Universitario Menéndez Pidal, Universidad Complutense de Madrid).

——, 2005. 'A Web-Implementation of Harriet Goldberg's Motif-Index of Folk Narratives in the Pan-Hispanic Romancero', in *'Entra mayo y sale abril': Medieval Spanish Literary and Folklore Studies in Memory of Harriet Goldberg*, ed. Manuel Da Costa Fontes & Joseph T. Snow, Juan de la Cuesta Hispanic Monographs, Homenajes, 25 (Newark, Delaware: Juan de la Cuesta), pp. 303–19.

PIÑERO RAMÍREZ, Pedro M. et al, ed., 2001. *La eterna agonía del romancero: Homenaje a Paul Bénichou*, De viva voz, 3 (Sevilla: Fundación Machado).

——, 2004. *Romancero de la Provincia de Huelva*, Romancero general de Andalucía, 2 (Huelva: Diputación de Huelva, Fundación Machado).

RODRÍGUEZ PUÉRTOLAS, Julio, 1972. 'El romancero, historia de una frustración', *Philological Quarterly*, 51: 85–104.

SÁNCHEZ-ROMERALO, Antonio, 1979. 'Razón y sinrazón en la creación tradicional', in *El Romancero hoy*, ed. Catalán et al 1979, II, pp. 13–28.

SILVERMAN, Joseph H., 1979. 'La contaminación como arte en un romance sefardí de Tánger', in *El Romancero hoy*, ed. Catalán et al 1979, II, pp. 29–37.

SMITH, Colin, 1970. *Ramón Menéndez Pidal, 1869–1968*, Diamante, 19 (London: The Hispanic & Luso-Brazilian Councils).

——, 1972. 'On the Ethos of the Romancero viejo', in *Studies of the Spanish and Portuguese Ballad* by N. D. Shergold (London: Tamesis with Univ. of Wales Press), pp. 5–24.

——, ed., 1996. *Spanish Ballads*, 2nd edn (Bristol: Classical Press).

SPONSLER, Lucy, 1975. *Women in the Medieval Spanish Epic & Lyric Traditions*, Studies in Romance Languages, 13 (Lexington: Kentucky UP).

SUÁREZ ROBAINA, Juana Rosa, 2003. *El personaje mujer en el romancero tradicional: imagen, amor y ubicación* (Las Palmas de Gran Canaria: Ediciones del Cabildo de Gran Canaria).

SZERTICS, Joseph, 1967. *Tiempo y verbo en el romancero viejo* (Madrid: Gredos).

TRAPERO, Maximiano, 1989. *Romancero tradicional canario*, Biblioteca básica canaria, 2 (Islas Canarias: Viceconsejería de Cultura y Deportes, Gobierno de Canarias).

——, 2003. *Romancero de la Gomera y el romancero general a comienzos del tercer milenio* (Madrid: Gredos).

VALENCIANO, Ana, 1989. 'Survival of the Traditional Romancero', in Webber 1989: 26–52.

VASVÁRI, Louise, 1999. *The Heterotextual Body of the 'Mora Morilla'*, PMHRS, 12 (London: Department of Hispanic Studies: Queen Mary and Westfield College).

WEBBER, Ruth House, 1951. *Formulistic Diction in the Spanish Ballad* (Berkeley: University of California Press).

——, 1989. *Hispanic Balladry Today*, The Albert Bates Lord Studies in Oral Tradition, 3, Garland Reference Library of the Humanities, 765 (New York: Garland).

WILSON, Edward M., 1958. *Tragic Themes in Spanish Ballads*, Diamante, 8 (London: Hispanic & Luso-Brazilian Councils).

WRIGHT, Roger, 1986. 'How Old is the Ballad Genre?', *C*, 14: 251–57.

——, ed. & tr., *Spanish Ballads with English Verse Translations* (Warminster: Aris & Phillips).

——, 1989–90. 'Several Ballads, One Epic and Two Chronicles', *C*, 18: 21–37.

——, 1991. *Spanish Ballads*, Critical Guides to Spanish Texts, 52 (London: Grant & Cutler).

——, 2000. 'Point of View in the Ballad Performer', *Hispanic Research Journal*, 1: 97–104.

——, 2004. 'Spanish Ballads in a Changing World', in *The Singer and the Scribe: European Ballad Traditions and European Ballad Cultures*, ed. Philip E. Bennett & Richard Firth Green (New York: Rodopi), pp. 169–81.

ZADERENKO, Irene, 2005. 'Épica y romancero del Cid', C, 33: 231–45.

Menéndez Pidal and Alphonsine Historiography

David G. Pattison

(*Magdalen College, Oxford*)

Any discussion of the complex and at first sight impenetrable subject of Alphonsine historiography tends to start with one of two well worn metaphors. Here are both of them. Menéndez Pidal himself used the Dantesque one of 'una selva selvaggia e aspra e forte' (Menéndez Pidal 1955: 137), and an early editor of one chronicle, the Marqués de la Fuensanta del Valle, opened his nineteenth-century edition with the laconic remark 'Decir crónicas es decir laberinto' (Fuensanta del Valle 1893: v).

To open a way into this forest or labyrinth I have chosen first to describe the achievements of Menéndez Pidal and of other work done during his lifetime; and to follow this with a brief account of what has been done in the last forty years. In each case I feel it is helpful to try to divide the material into three aspects of dealing with chronicle texts: classification; edition; and interpretation: while, of course, admitting that most scholars working in the field have tackled more than one of these aspects, often in the same publication.

This is axiomatically true of the very first of Menéndez Pidal's published work in this area, *La Leyenda de los Infantes de Lara*, which first appeared in 1896. Over one hundred and ten years ago, Menéndez Pidal gave us a masterly essay on the relationship of relevant chronicle versions and an edition of the appropriate parts of one of them; and, for the interpretative side, developed and exemplified the theory of reconstruction of lost epic texts from the historiographic prose. At the same time he was developing the classification of manuscripts which was to see the light over fifty years afterwards but which was there in essence in his 1898 monograph *Crónicas generales de España*, now best known in its third amplified edition of 1918. And, in 1906, there appeared what must at the time have appeared to be the definitive edition of 'the' text of the Alphonsine enterprise, under the title *Primera Crónica General*. That title is now relatively little used except as a handy way of referring to Menéndez Pidal's published edition. The preferred designation is now *Estoria de España* (which, incidentally, also appeared on the title page in 1906, though in a subsidiary position, as sub-title).

As for the 'interpretation' heading, that is best seen, in these early years, in the 1923 article 'Relatos poéticos en las crónicas medievales', which established the orthodox view that chroniclers used epic poems as sources for their narratives and that these lost poems can in fact be reconstructed from the prose texts. This aspect of Menéndez Pidal's work, adumbrated in *La Leyenda de los Infantes de Lara*, reached its apogee in *Reliquias de la poesía épica española*, first published in 1951 though going back to work done before the Civil War, some of which was published in *Historia y epopeya* (1934), some prepared as *Epopeya y romancero*, but whose publication was interrupted by the conflict.

Finally, in 1955, Menéndez Pidal published a second edition of his 1906 *Primera Crónica General*, adding a long and detailed 'Estudio' of 70 pages, and in the same year returned to the question of classification in his article 'Tradicionalidad de las Crónicas Generales de España'.

Before going on to look at the work of Menéndez Pidal's successors, a minor point may be made. Most people are familiar with his definition of the *romancero* as 'poesía que vive en variantes'; in the 1955 article just referred to, he quoted Lindley Cintra in drawing a parallel between this state of *variación* and something similar in the case of chronicle versions:

> Como los poemas épicos, como los romances, la historiografía fué, durante la Edad Media, un género tradicional en las literaturas peninsulares; la diferencia estaba en que, en el caso de las gestas y romances, la transmisión era oral, en las crónicas era escrita (Menéndez Pidal 1955: 137, translating Lindley Cintra 1951–90, I: cccxvi).

I should like to take this comparison a stage further and to point out that Menéndez Pidal's own work can be seen, by a careful attention to its descriptive bibliography, to have evolved in a similar state of 'tradicionalidad': consider the publishing history of *La Leyenda de los Infantes de Lara*, from 1896, to a second edition in 1934 containing additions including a much fuller catalogue of chronicle manuscripts, to the 1971 re-edition by Diego Catalán with two further sets of new material dating from 1950–51 and 1968. Likewise, the *Primera Crónica General*, as already described, reappeared in 1955, the text unchanged but with the addition of a newly published 'Estudio' which owed much to work done in the early years of the century; the same material, including the 1955 'Estudio' was republished in 1977 as the first two volumes of *Fuentes Cronísticas de la Historia de España*, with a title page stating that they contained 'un estudio actualizador' by Diego Catalán; however, this study, advertised as a third volume, did not appear, 'por exigencias presupuestarias'; it is probable that the material, or some of it, resurfaced in Diego Catalán's 1997 book *De la silva textual al Taller Historiográfico Alfonsí*, to be mentioned below. A third case is *Reliquias de la poesía épica española*, of 1951, which re-appeared in 1980 with not only fresh introductory material by Diego Catalán but also the ur-text of *Epopeya y romancero* dating from the 1920s and 1930s. To complete this picture, it may be noted that in 1992 there appeared the book *La épica medieval española...*, a posthumous publication edited by Diego Catalán and María del Mar de Bustos. It contains much of the material dating from Menéndez Pidal's research in the 1930s and later, and includes chapters of great relevance for historiographic studies, notably those on Fernán González, the Condesa Traidora, the Infante García (here called 'el último conde de Castilla') and Sancho II (here 'Sancho el fuerte'). There is, in short, a constant process of revision and variation going on, analogous to that which Menéndez Pidal himself identified in the 'selva selvaggia' or 'laberinto' of the manuscripts.

While Menéndez Pidal's work was evolving in the sixty years from 1896 onwards, what else was happening in the field of Spanish chronicle studies? The most significant contribution, with hindsight, was probably the work done in the 1930s by the American Theodore Babbitt. In a short series of articles and a book published in 1936 he took one chronicle version — the so-called *Crónica de Veinte Reyes* — and made a systematic comparison of its text with that published in 1906 by Menéndez Pidal, showing, basically, that in a number of aspects the *Crónica de Veinte Reyes* seemed to reflect an earlier version of the narrative than that of the so-called *'Primera' Crónica*. Babbitt's conclusions were, it is true, vitiated by the fact that he was too apt to see the two chronicles — *Primera Crónica General* and *Crónica de Veinte Reyes* — as 'texts', and at the same time there was too little appreciation of the essential variability among manuscripts (something which Menéndez Pidal took up in his 1955 article); it is therefore easy to characterise Babbitt's view as simplistic. But his work was thoughtful and careful, and also courageous in a way which now can seem anachronistic to those who do not recall how difficult it could be, in a Hispanic context, to challenge received orthodoxy and authority.

A second American, who was doing valuable work in the 1950s and 1960s was Samuel Armistead, although, apart from a handful of short articles, the fruits of his work on the epic tradition of the *Mocedades de Rodrigo* and its reflection in the so-called *Crónica de Castilla*, was published only in 2000. His 1955 Princeton doctoral dissertation, though, shows how much he too was challenging accepted orthodoxy and ensuring that later chronicle versions were taken into account.

The same is true of my next example, the Portuguese scholar Luis Felipe Lindley Cintra, already mentioned, who, also in the 1950s, embarked on the edition of the *Crónica de 1344* in its original Portuguese version. The first three volumes appeared between 1951 and 1955 (the fourth only in 1990), and of these the first contained a 571-page 'Introdução' which tackled the questions of classification and relationships among versions in a way comparable in thoroughness and sophistication to Menéndez Pidal's own work (Menéndez Pidal's 1955 article 'Tradicionalidad de las Crónicas Generales de España' to which I have referred was conceived as a review-article of Lindley Cintra's work, although it can be said to have outgrown this genesis).

Other scholars worked on aspects which fall more into my category of 'interpretation': work done on the legends of Bernardo del Carpio by the German Heinermann in 1927 and the American Franklin in 1937, on Fernán González by the Dutch Sneyders de Vogel in 1923, and, in Oxford, on Cidian materials by Entwistle (1947) and Russell (1958).

As for chronicle editions, apart from Lindley Cintra's work the only pre-1960 item of note was an edition of Juan Manuel's *Crónica Abreviada* (an index to the lost version known as the *Crónica Manuelina*), published in 1958 by Raymond and Mildred Grismer in the U.S.A.

In Spain, matters began to progress in the early 1960s. The librarian José Gómez Pérez published three substantial articles between 1959 and 1965 in which he began to explore some of the complexities of the manuscript tradition and the relationships between variant chronicle versions, covering some of the same ground as Babbitt had done twenty-five years previously. Of absolutely capital importance, however, was the appearance, in 1962, of the book by Diego Catalán, Menéndez Pidal's grandson, *De Alfonso X al Conde de Barcelos*. This truly ground-breaking study represented the first sustained critique to be published in Spanish — though one should not forget Lindley Cintra's 1951 Portuguese study — of the relationships existing among the numerous manuscripts of the 'laberinto'. It is to Diego Catalán that we owe the first proper evaluation of the importance and relationships of such versions as the *Crónica General 'Vulgata'*, the *Crónica Ocampiana*, the *Crónica de 1344*, and others. However, the most striking aspect of the book was Diego Catalán's demonstration that the manuscript used as a base text for his grandfather's edition of the supposedly *'Primera' Crónica General* was in fact a relatively late and idiosyncratic variant of the 'versión regia' and that the so-called 'versión vulgar' (showing some similarities and points of contact with, among other versions, the *Crónica de Veinte Reyes*) might represent a more primitive and more authentically Alphonsine stage in the evolution of the chronicle. Diego Catalán followed up the book with a series of articles — of which I give only three significant examples in the list of works cited, between 1963 and 1969 — elaborating his ideas and applying them to problems in the interpretation of the chronicle material and in many cases to the vexed question of use of historiographic material in the reconstruction of supposedly lost epic texts. These articles and others are reprinted, integrally or in part, in Diego Catalán's 1992 book *La Estoria de España de Alfonso X: Creación y evolución*.

In 1967 the British Hispanist Derek Lomax, contributing to the Modern Humanities Research Association's *Year's Work in Modern Language Studies*, commented 'J. Gómez Pérez and D. Catalán continue to stalk each other through the undergrowth of General Chronicles' (Lomax 1967: 179), and went on to ask whether the most urgent requirement was not the edition of more chronicle manuscripts rather than typological studies whose accuracy could not be properly assessed in the absence of available texts. In fact the process of editing texts has been relatively slow — or at least *was* very slow for twenty years after Lomax made his plea. In 1971 Diego Catalán, in collaboration with María Soledad de Andrés, began the publication of the Castilian version of the *Crónica de 1344*, but this never got beyond the first volume. In 1975–77 Ramón Lorenzo published a Galician translation of the *Crónica General* and the *Crónica de Castilla*. There were partial editions of some other minor chronicles (e.g., the American Thomas Lathrop, in 1971, edited an idiosyncratic version of the story of the Infantes de Lara in what is called the *Refundición Toledana de la Crónica de 1344*, a fifteenth-century text); and the British hispanist Brian Powell, whose work I shall discuss below, gave us, in 1983, an edition of that section of the *Crónica de veinte reyes* corresponding to the narrative contained in the *Poema de mio Cid*; and that is basically how things stood until the 1990s.

Before looking at the important work done in that decade, chiefly by disciples of Diego Catalán, among whose work that of Inés Fernández-Ordóñez stands out, let me briefly sketch what went on in the fields of classification and interpretation outside Spain. In this country, the two names to mention are those of Brian Powell and myself. Both of us, working quite independently, published books with similar titles in the same year, 1983. They are rather different. Powell's was called *Epic and Chronicle: The 'Poema de mio Cid' and the 'Crónica de veinte reyes'*. Its sub-title points to the fact that — as well as the partial edition of the *Crónica de veinte reyes* already mentioned — the book consists of a detailed comparison of the *Poema de mio Cid* and the *Crónica de veinte reyes*. The background to this, as Powell also sets out, is that of all the chronicle versions that of the *Crónica de veinte reyes* is manifestly the closest to the surviving poetic text. Where other chronicles — such as the *Primera Crónica General* — differ, it was Menéndez Pidal's view that they were based on a variant form: a *refundición* of the *Poema*. Powell's conclusion deserves brief quotation:

> Variations in stories cannot simply be attributed to variable poetic texts which came to the notice of different chroniclers at different times. In most cases, variations from one chronicle to another are due to the chroniclers, who intervened more in the transmission of their sources than has been thought (Powell 1983: 111).

This was not in itself original: some of Diego Catalán's articles from the 1960s, most specifically the 1969 'Poesía y novela en la historiografía castellana' had been tending in the same direction. And this was the theme of my own 1983 book, *From Legend to Chronicle*, where, after examining a range of epic legends in their chronicle versions, I argued that where 'a story containing substantially new elements, differs from the version prosified in other chronicles, in prose which contains strong traces of assonance' (Pattison 1983: 145), there may be a case for the postulation of a *refundición*, a more developed version of the original poem; but in a great number of other cases, chroniclers may be assumed to have rewritten their sources in line with their views of verisimilitude, propriety, consistency, and other criteria. This aspect is very much in line with Powell's conclusions, which are based on the one instance in which we are actually able to compare an extant poetic text with its prose chronicle version.

I continued to work in the area of chronicles for some years after 1983, producing analyses of versions such as the *Crónica Abreviada* of Don Juan Manuel (1992) and the *Crónica Ocampiana* (1993), as well as making one modest discovery in the British Library, where I believe I found a fragmentary text of the lost *Crónica Manuelina*, of which the *Abreviada* is an index or summary (1992).

Elsewhere in Europe, the 1976 book by the Belgian Louis Chalon, *L'Histoire et l'épopée castillane du moyen âge* looked at a similar range of legends to those studied seven years later by me, but, as the title implies, the Belgian author was more concerned with tracing historical than with legendary connections, while at the same time contributing to our understanding of the relationships among chronicle families. In France the importance of the interpretative contribution of Georges Martin cannot be exaggerated. In the words of Fernando Gómez Redondo,

> Con presupuestos semiológicos y textuales, ha desbrozado una de las líneas interpretativas más sugerentes de la historiografía medieval, demostrando que la crónica es un 'discurso histórico' que refleja la 'mentalidad' y la ideología de su promotor, constituyendo un ámbito de reconstrucción de la épica y del romancero (Gómez Redondo 1998–2007, I: 652).

This is based chiefly on Martin's 1992 book *Les Juges de Castille*, and also on the later *Histoires de l'Espagne médiévale* (1997). It should be added that Martin shows signs of having created a 'school' of researchers, an example of whose work I have included in the list of works cited under the name of Marta Lacomba, whose 2006 article follows on neatly both from Martin's own more theoretical perspectives and the ideas put forward twenty years ago by Powell and myself.

In North America relatively little has been done since the pioneering work of Samuel Armistead in the 1950s and 1960s, already referred to; Nancy Joe Dyer, working in the 1970s, examined the prosification of the *Poema de mio Cid* in the *Primera Crónica General* and the *Crónica de Veinte Reyes*, and, like Powell, gave us a partial edition of the text of the latter chronicle, though hers was not published until 1995. Charles Fraker did valuable and suggestive work in the 1970s and 1980s, chiefly on the early stages of the Cid's career and the reign of Sancho II, and these were re-published in 1997 in the author's *The Scope of History*. In South America, the work of Leonardo Funes in Buenos Aires has developed narratological models which, in Fernando Gómez Redondo's words, serve to 'verificar el funcionamiento de sus ideas y de sus núcleos temáticos engastados en el modelo cultural que promueve Alfonso X' (Gómez Redondo 1998–2007, I: 653).

As for work in Spain, I have been at pains to point out that the single most important figure in Alphonsine historiographic studies after Ramón Menéndez Pidal was his grandson, Diego Catalán, whose recent death this colloquium commemorates. The ground-breaking book of 1962 and the series of equally important articles of the later 1960s and 1970s, collected in book form in 1992, plus the re-editing and amplification of his grandfather's work — *La Leyenda de los Infantes de Lara* in 1971, *Primera Crónica General* in 1977, *Reliquias de la poesía épica española* in 1980 — were complemented by a further series of important contributions in the 1990s, reaching something of a summation in the 1997 publication *De la silva textual al Taller Historiográfico Alfonsí*, whose subtitle, *Códices, crónicas, versiones y cuadernos de trabajo* gives some idea of its scope.

However, as well as his own work, Diego Catalán was instrumental, through institutions, all bearing the name of Menéndez Pidal, the Fundación, the Instituto Universitario Seminario, and the Centro de Estudios Históricos, in co-ordinating and promoting the work of a team of younger scholars, of whom the best known is perhaps Inés Fernández-Ordóñez. She is the editor of what is undoubtedly the major discovery of the post-Pidalian period, published in 1993, one of the manuscripts held in the Caja de Ahorros de Salamanca, which has been baptised with the name *Versión Crítica de la Estoria de España*. This version was described in Fernando Gómez Redondo's words as being 'la última redacción aprobada por Alfonso en el período de 1282–84'. Gómez Redondo goes on to describe this discovery as 'piedra angular de un nuevo planteamiento investigador', and says that work by this team of researchers 'ha modificado, de forma absoluta, todas las ideas recibidas sobre la historiografía alfonsí' (Gómez Redondo 1998–2007, I: 651). It would be invidious not to mention others in the team, Mariano de la Campa, Juan Bautista Crespo, Joaquín Rubio Tovar, and María del Mar de Bustos, the last-named having produced an edition, of the *Crónica General 'Vulgata'* (an as yet unpublished doctoral thesis) in 1994. Inés Fernández-Ordóñez, in addition to the valuable editorial work referred to, has been active in writing and organising collaborative work in the area, most notably the volume *Alfonso X el Sabio y las Crónicas de España*, which appeared in 2000.

I will finish by referring to a review article I wrote in 1995 entitled 'New Perspectives in Alphonsine Historiography'; the books which gave me a stepping-off point were Diego Catalán's 1992 collection *La Estoria de España de Alfonso X: Creación y evolución*, and Inés Fernández-Ordóñez's edition (1993) of the *Versión crítica*. I there quoted Derek Lomax's 1967 plea (see above. p. 87) for more chronicle editions, and went on, 'Given the complexities of the manuscript tradition, that has always been a counsel of perfection. It is clear, though, that progress is being made in the right direction; the continued work of the Seminario Menéndez Pidal […] shows that chronicle studies in Spain are in good hands. Dr Fernández-Ordóñez, who pays fulsome tribute to the inspiration and example of Diego Catalán, is a worthy inheritor of the tradition stretching back to Ramón Menéndez Pidal' (Pattison 1995: 289).

Works Cited

Armistead, Samuel G., 1955. *'La gesta de las Mocedades de Rodrigo': Reflections of a lost epic poem in the 'Crónica de los reyes de Castilla' and the 'Crónica de 1344'* (unpublished doctoral dissertation, Princeton University).

——, *La tradición épica de las 'Mocedades de Rodrigo'* (Salamanca: Universidad, 2000).

Babbitt, Theodore, 1936. *La Crónica de Veinte Reyes: A comparison with the text of the Primera Crónica General and a study of the principal Latin sources* (New Haven: Yale University Press).

Bustos, María del Mar de, 1994. *La 'Crónica General Vulgata'*, (unpublished doctoral dissertation, Universidad Autónoma de Madrid).

Catalán, Diego, 1962. *De Alfonso X al Conde de Barcelos: Cuatro estudios sobre el nacimiento de la historiografía romance en Castilla y Portugal* (Madrid: Gredos/Seminario Menéndez Pidal).

——, 1963a. 'Crónicas generales y cantares de gesta: El *Mio Cid* de Alfonso X y el del pseudo Ben Alfaraŷ', *HR*, 31: 195–215, 291–306.

——, 1963b. 'El taller historiográfico alfonsí: Métodos y problemas en el trabajo compilatorio', *Romania*, 84: 354–75.

——, 1969. 'Poesía y novela en la historiografía castellana de los siglos XIII y XIV' in *Mélanges offerts à Rita Lejeune*, I (Gembloux: Duculot), pp. 423–41.

——, 1992. *La 'Estoria de España' de Alfonso X: Creación y evolución*, FCHE, 5 (Madrid: Fundación Menéndez Pidal/Universidad Autónoma).

——, 1997. *De la Silva Textual al Taller Historiográfico Alfonsí: Códices, crónicas, versiones y cuadernos de trabajo*, FCHE, 9 (Madrid: Fundación Menéndez Pidal/Universidad Autónoma).

——, & María Soledad de Andrés, eds., 1971. *Crónica General de España de 1344*, I, FCHE, 2 (Madrid: Gredos/Seminario Menéndez Pidal).

Chalon, Louis, 1976. *L'Histoire et l'épopée castillane du moyen âge* (Paris: Champion).

Dyer, Nancy Joe, 1995. *El 'Mio Cid' del taller alfonsí* (Newark, Delaware: Juan de la Cuesta).

Entwistle, William J., 1947. 'La Estoria del Noble Varón el Çid Ruy Díaz el Campeador, sennor que fue de Valencia', *HR*, 15: 206–11.

Fernández-Ordóñez, Inés, ed. 1993. *Versión Crítica de la 'Estoria de España': Estudio y Edición desde Pelayo hasta Ordoño II*, FCHE, 6 (Madrid: Fundación Menéndez Pidal/Universidad Autónoma).

——, ed., 2000. *Alfonso X el Sabio y las Crónicas de España* (Valladolid: Universidad/ Centro para la Edición de los Clásicos Españoles).

Fraker, Charles F., 1974. 'Sancho II: Epic and Chronicle', *Romania*, 95: 467–507; reprinted in the author's *The Scope of History: Studies in the Historiography of Alfonso el Sabio*, 1996 (Ann Arbor: University of Michigan), pp. 44–84.

FRANKLIN, Albert B., III, 1937. 'A Study of the Origins of the Legend of Bernardo del Carpio', *HR* 5: 286–303.

FUENSANTA DEL VALLE, Marqués de la, 1893. *Crónica de España del Arzobispo don Rodrigo Jiménez de Rada*, Colección de Documentos Inéditos para la Historia de España, 105 (Madrid: printed by José Perales).

FUNES, Leonardo, 1997. *El modelo historiográfico alfonsí: una caracterización*, PMHRS, 6 (London: Queen Mary & Westfield College).

GÓMEZ PÉREZ, José, 1959. 'Fuentes y cronología en la *Primera crónica general de España*', *RABM*, 67: 615–34.

——, 1963. 'Elaboración de la *Primera crónica general de España* y su trasmisión manuscrita', *Scriptorium*, 17: 233–76.

——, 1965. 'La *Estoria de España* de Fruela II a Fernando III', *Hispania*, 25: 481–520.

GÓMEZ REDONDO, Fernando, 1998–2007. *Historia de la prosa medieval castellana*, 4 vols., (Madrid: Cátedra).

GRISMER, Raymond L., & Mildred B., eds. 1958. *Juan Manuel, Crónica Abreviada* (Minneapolis: Burgess).

HEINERMANN, Th., 1927. *Untersuchungen zur Entstehung der Sage von Bernardo del Carpio* (Halle: Niemeyer).

LACOMBA, Marta, 2006. 'L'utilisation des *cantares* et la notion de vérité dans la *Version de ca 1283* de l'*Estoria de España*: le recours à l'*argumentum* comme critère de définition du vraisemblable', *Cahiers d'études hispaniques médiévales*, 29: 265–76.

LATHROP, Thomas A., 1971. *The Legend of the 'Siete Infantes de Lara' (Refundición toledana de la crónica de 1344 version)* (Chapel Hill: University of North Carolina).

LINDLEY CINTRA, Luis Felipe, ed., 1951–90. *Crónica Geral de Espanha de 1344*, 4 vols. (Lisbon: Academia Portuguesa da História).

LOMAX, Derek W., 1967. 'Spanish Studies: Medieval Literature', *Year's Work in Modern Language Studies*, 29: 172–85.

LORENZO, Ramón, ed., 1975–77. *La traducción gallega de la Crónica General y de la Crónica de Castilla*, 2 vols. (Orense: Instituto de Estudios Orensanos).

MARTIN, Georges, 1992. *Les juges de Castille: Mentalités et discours historique dans l'Espagne médiévale* (Paris: Klincksieck).

——, 1997. *Histoires de l'Espagne médiévale: Historiographie, geste, romancero* (Paris: Klincksieck).

MENÉNDEZ PIDAL, Ramón, 1896. *La leyenda de los Infantes de Lara* (Madrid: author, printed by Hijos de José M. Ducazcal); 2a edn. with 'Adiciones', 1934 (Madrid: Hernando); 3a edn., ed. Diego Catalán with 'Adiciones de 1950–51 y 1968', 1971 (Madrid: Espasa-Calpe).

——, 1898. *Crónicas generales de España*, Catálogo de la Real Biblioteca, 5 (Madrid: Rivadeneyra), 3a edn. 'con notables enmiendas, adiciones y mejoras', 1918 (Madrid: Blass).

——, ed. 1906. *Primera Crónica General: Estoria de España que mandó componer Alfonso el Sabio y se continuaba bajo Sancho IV en 1289*, NBAE, 5 (Madrid:

Bailly-Baillière); 2a edn., *Primera Crónica General que mandó componer...* with 'Estudio' and 'Fuentes', 2 vols., 1955 (Madrid: Gredos); 3a edn., ed. Diego Catalán, with 'Estudio (1955) as 'Apéndice'; the 'Estudio actualizador' by Diego Catalán, promised as vol. 3, did not appear; 2 vols., FCHE, 1–2, 1977 (Madrid: Fundación Menéndez Pidal/Universidad Autónoma).
——, 1923. 'Relatos poéticos en las crónicas medievales', *RFE*, 10: 329–72.
——, 1934. *Historia y epopeya* (Madrid: Hernando).
——, ed. 1951. *Reliquias de la poesía épica española* (Madrid: Espasa-Calpe); 2a edn., *...acompañadas de 'Epopeya y romancero I'*, ed. Diego Catalán, 1980 (Madrid: Gredos/Cátedra-Seminario Menéndez Pidal).
——, 1955. 'Tradicionalidad de las Crónicas Generales de España', *BRAH*, 136: 131–97.
——, 1992. *La épica medieval española desde sus orígenes hasta su disolución en el romancero*, eds. Diego Catalán & María del Mar de Bustos (Madrid: Espasa-Calpe).
Pattison, David G., 1983. *From Legend to Chronicle: The treatment of epic material in Alphonsine historiography*, MA Monographs (New Series), XIII (Oxford: SSMLL).
——, 1992a. 'British Library Ms. Egerton 289: A glimpse of the *Cronica Manuelina*', *C*, 21.1: 15–30.
——, 1992b. 'Juan Manuel's *Crónica Abreviada* and Alphonsine historiography', *MA*, 61: 242–49.
——, 1993. 'The *Crónica Ocampiana*: a reappraisal', in *Letters and Society in Fifteenth-Century Spain: Studies presented to P. E. Russell on his Eightieth Birthday*, ed. Alan Deyermond & Jeremy Lawrance ([Llangranog]: Dolphin Book Co.), pp. 137–47.
——, 1995. 'New Perspectives in Alphonsine Historiography' (review article), *MA*, 64: 285–90.
Powell, Brian, 1983. *Epic and Chronicle: The 'Poema de mio Cid' and the 'Crónica de veinte reyes'*, MHRA Texts and Dissertations, 18 (London: MHRA).
Russell, Peter E., 1958. 'San Pedro de Cardeña and the Heroic History of the Cid', *MA*, 27: 57–79.
Sneyders de Vogel, K., 1923. 'Le *Poema de Fernán González* et la *Crónica General*', *Neophilologus*, 8: 161–80.

In Search of the Eternal Nation: Ramón Menéndez Pidal and the History of Spain

SIMON BARTON
(*University of Exeter*)

It is actually something of a paradox. It is as a philologist and as a literary scholar, rather than as a historian, that Ramón Menéndez Pidal (1869–1968) is probably best remembered today, yet the colossus of twentieth-century Hispanic Studies devoted a good part of his extraordinarily long and intellectually fertile career to the study of history. It is also arguable that of all his voluminous writings it was his historical research that had the greatest impact on the society of his day.

The importance that Menéndez Pidal attached to the study of history and his appreciation of the influence of the past on the creation of a distinctive Spanish cultural identity is writ large throughout most of his scholarly endeavours (García Isasti 2004: 74–83). It can be seen, for example, in his painstaking textual study of Alfonsine historiography, which culminated in his edition of what he called the *Primera Crónica General* in 1906; in the overtly historicist approach he adopted to the Castilian epic, most notably in his pioneering editions of *La Leyenda de los Infantes de Lara* (1896) and the *Cantar de Mio Cid* (1908–11);[1] and in his monumental study of Spanish linguistics, the *Orígenes del Español* (1926). Menéndez Pidal devoted a number of influential essays to historical themes during the course of his career, but his reputation as a historian rests above all on three major works: *La España del Cid* (1929), *Los españoles en la historia* (1947) and *El Padre Las Casas: su doble personalidad* (1963). In this article I propose to subject these works to scrutiny and examine what it was that prompted Menéndez Pidal to write history in the first place,

---

[1] 'Pidal concibe el estudio de la épica como algo absolutamente entrelazado con el estudio de la historia medieval, en ambos casos a través del descubrimiento y crítica de fuentes documentales de época, que se utilizarán complementariamente en estudios históricos y filológicos. Dicho en otras palabras, Pidal no concibe ninguna frontera sustancial entre ambas disciplinas académicas, la Historia y la Filología' (García Isasti 2004: 75)

the methodology he adopted in the course of his research, and the ideological concerns that underpinned his scholarly enterprises in this field.

La España del Cid

Without any doubt Menéndez Pidal's most influential work of history was *La España del Cid*, a detailed biography of the life and times of Rodrigo Díaz de Vivar, the Cid, published by Espasa-Calpe in 1929, when don Ramón was already at the summit of his profession and at the peak of his intellectual powers. The work was the culmination of more than two decades of research on the Castilian warrior hero, during the course of which Menéndez Pidal had completed his acclaimed edition of the *Cantar de Mio Cid*. His stated aims in writing the work were manifold. First, there was his general concern that the remarkable deeds of the Cid had been neglected by his countrymen and were in danger of being forgotten, and thus he declared his determination to restore the hero to his rightful place in the collective national historical memory:

> Me propongo, sobre todo, depurar y reavivir el recuerdo del Cid, que, siendo de los más consunstanciales y formativos del pueblo español, está entre nosotros muy necesitado de renovación. Porque es el caso que España, después de haber mantenido con amor ese gran recuerdo histórico a través de las edades, ahora hace más de un siglo que lo ha dejado perder, salvo en el terreno de la pura poesía [...] Pensando en esto cuando escribía mi libro, sentí que al inicial interés histórico se añadía algo de interés piadoso (I, ix).

In this way, Menéndez Pidal spoke modestly of raising his own 'sencilla estela conmemorativa' to the Cid (I, ix).

But *La España del Cid* was far more than simply an act of scholarly *pietas*. It had an overtly polemical edge too. At one level, Menéndez Pidal designed his book to be a decisive, withering riposte to what he considered to be the malicious and hostile portraits of the Cid that had been penned by the Catalan Jesuit Juan Francisco Masdeu (1805), who had even denied the Cid's very existence, and subsequently by the Dutch orientalist, Reinhart Dozy (1849). It had been Dozy who, by scrutinising a number of largely unknown Arabic texts, not least a then recently discovered work of Ibn Bassam, had sought to disentangle the Cid of legend from the Cid of history and had called into question the mythical status that the Castilian noble had acquired in Spain by that time. Far from being a champion of Christendom, Dozy had argued, the Cid was a pragmatic mercenary, a despoiler of churches, a perjurer, a man without principles or piety, more Muslim than Catholic in his beliefs. Dozy's scholarly assault on one of Spain's own national treasures, which as Richard Fletcher aptly put it 'tossed a bomb into the cosy arena of national hagiography and Romantic blather' (Fletcher 1989: 200), caused anger and stupefaction in equal part in the Cid's homeland. But until Menéndez Pidal took up cudgels on the Cid's behalf no one had had the necessary intellectual firepower to dare take on the erudite Dozy. In *La España del Cid* Menéndez Pidal utterly rejected Dozy's portrait of the 'historical Cid', suggesting that the Dutch scholar's work, like that of Masdeu before him, owed more to malevolence, to full-blown 'Cidofobia', than to dispassionate scholarly analysis:

> El saber erudito de Dozy es amigo encubierto de la cidofobia [...] "le Cid de la realité" que nos trazó Dozy es tan poco real, como el Cid de los poetas de la baja Edad Media [...] los moros no falsearon el tipo de su enemigo, y sí lo falseó el doctísimo profesor de Leiden (I, 44).

Instead, Menéndez Pidal warned that if the 'verdadero Cid' (I, 31) were to be discovered he would need to get back to basics: 'Hemos de reconstruir la biografía desde sus cimientos' (I, 45); but he warned that 'edificamos sobre un terreno arenoso [...] sobre un terreno enaguado por la admiración, enfangado por el odio' (I, 52).

However, Menéndez Pidal intended his work to be far more than a simple piece of robust academic polemic. There was a didactic purpose too. Writing in the dying days of the Primo de Rivera dictatorship, a time when the regime was facing mounting opposition from liberal politicians, intellectuals, regional nationalists and working class groups, among others, Menéndez Pidal hoped that at a time when, as he put it, military virtues were no longer so admired by contemporaries, his work might have a greater resonance among the society of his day:

> Y aún la vida del Cid tiene, como no podía menos, una especial oportunidad española ahora, época de desaliento entre

nosotros, en que el escepticismo ahoga los sentimientos de solidaridad y la insolidaridad alimenta al escepticismo. Contra esta debilidad actual del espíritu colectivo pudieran servir de reacción todos los grandes recuerdos históricos que más nos hacen intimar con la esencia del pueblo a que pertenecemos y que más pueden robustecer aquella trabazón de los espíritus – el alma colectiva –, inspiradora de la cohesion social (I, viii–ix).

In short, Menéndez Pidal believed, passionately, that just as the creators of the medieval epic in times past had sought to inspire their audiences to imitate the deeds of great heroes like the Cid, so the discipline of history could in turn perform a similar didactic function among the Spaniards of his day. As he had earlier commented at the end of his short work *El Cid en la historia* of 1921:

Y siempre la vida del Campeador será alto ejemplo que nos hará concebir la nuestra como regida por un deber de actividad máxima; siempre requerirá de nosotros esa heroicidad obscura, anónima, diaria, única base firme de engrandecimiento de los pueblos y sin la cual el heroismo esplendente no tiene base; siempre nos guiará a nortear el supremo y último rumbo del interés personal hacia los ideales colectivos de la sociedad humana a que estamos ligados y dentro de la cual nuestra breve vida recibe un valor de eternidad (51–2).

For Menéndez Pidal, the study of history was relevant not just because it helped to bring the past alive, but because the shared collective memory of certain past events and an appreciation of the virtues and deeds of great men and women could also act as a kind of social glue, instilling a common patriotism, national unity and solidarity that could overcome regional, cultural or political differences.

La España del Cid displays the same formidable erudition and careful attention to detail that had been the hallmark of all Menéndez Pidal's textual studies hitherto and he buttressed his arguments with a hefty appendix of primary sources, including editions of the Latin *Carmen Campidoctoris* and the *Historia Roderici* and a collection of documents, which he dubbed the *cartulario cidiano* (II, 825–975). True to its title, Menéndez Pidal's work attempted far more than a mere biography of the Cid, but instead sought to place the career of the hero fully in the political and social context of his times. As far as methodology is concerned, what most raises eyebrows today is Menéndez Pidal's readiness to weave 'historical' and 'legendary' elements into a seamless whole, so that in many respects he accorded far more credence to the portrait of the Cid provided by the vernacular *Cantar*, which he dated to *c.*1140, than to the plainer, although probably more reliable, Latin prose *Historia Roderici*. Thus, for Pidal, poetic episodes such as 'la afrenta de Corpes', when the Cid's daughters were reputedly assaulted by the infantes de Carrión and left for dead, far from deriving from literary imagination, were events thoroughly grounded in fact. It is equally noteworthy that in his determination to uphold the reputation of the Cid at all costs, Menéndez Pidal agilely sidestepped the controversy surrounding his hero's devastating attack on Christian La Rioja in 1092 (I, 419–20), or his reported torture and execution of the former governor of Valencia, Ibn Jahhaf, in 1095 (II, 517–9). By contrast, Alfonso VI of León, for so long one of the most illustrious figures of Spanish historiography, was portrayed in an altogether more negative light (I, 409 ff.; Linehan 1993: 222–3).

Reduced to its essentials, *La España del Cid* rests upon three key arguments, all of which remain controversial to this day. The first was Menéndez Pidal's emphatic view that the 'Cid of history', far from being the hard-nosed mercenary that Dozy had claimed, had in fact remained a staunchly loyal vassal of his liege lord Alfonso VI of León throughout his career, his exile from Castile notwithstanding: 'su vida fue una constante fidelidad' (II, 596). Second, Menéndez Pidal argued vigorously that the rise of Castile during the later eleventh century at the expense of León marked a turning point in the creation, or rather re-creation, of Spain. Castile, he believed, was the motor of the Spanish *Reconquista* of Muslim-held territory, and the Cid was a willing and active agent of that programme of national solidarity and reunification:

> Las empresas cidianas en que cooperan caballeros de tantas regiones representan (aunque de iniciativa particular) el primero de esos amplios movimientos de solidaridad hispana que después se produjeron en los momentos más difíciles de la reconquista' (II, 608).

Finally, Menéndez Pidal viewed the Cid as a quasi-mystical figure, the archetypal Spaniard, whose virtues and heroic conduct in some way encapsulated the essential spirit of the Hispanic nation (García Isasti 2004: 117). By emphasising the primacy of national unity, of loyalty to the constituted authority, Menéndez Pidal sought to demonstrate to his fellow citizens the *modernidad* of the Cid, in the sense that driven by loyalty to the crown and a sense of patriotism, he was a man who, by protecting the Christian realms against Almoravid attacks, had acted for the good of the Hispanic nation and Europe as a whole (Lacarra 1980: 106, 113).

This thesis was itself underpinned by a series of ideolological substrata, which constituted the bedrock of Menéndez Pidal's 'historical vision', which he had already rehearsed during his American lecture tour of 1909 and in several published works thereafter (García Isasti 2004: 57–139). History, he believed, far from being a bare narrative of events, was something far more profound. Above all, there was his engrained belief in the eternal metaphysical nature of Spain, its *alma nacional* and the process of 'manifest destiny' that had guided its fortunes throughout history (García Isasti 2004). Coupled with this was his belief in the political and cultural hegemony of Castile, which had helped to restore the unity of Spain and to spread its power and culture around the globe thereafter. Keen to rebut the view that Spain constituted a 'people apart' in Europe, let alone a 'failed nation', as some were claiming at the time, Menéndez Pidal sought to demonstrate the essentially European character of the Spaniards — in terms of race, social organization and culture — despite the long hiatus caused by the Islamic conquest of the eighth century. As García Isasti has observed, 'no concibe su tarea como la de un frío y distante científico, sino como la de un patriota militante que trabaja por su país' (García Isasti 2004: 509–10).

Steven Hess has called *La España del Cid* 'the crown jewel among Pidal's historical studies' (Hess 1982: 69) and it is without doubt the work whose influence on subsequent generations was greatest, so much so that the book ran into seven editions, the most recent of them published by Espasa-Calpe in 1969, the year after Menéndez Pidal's death. Contemporaries were no less convinced of its importance. For Azorín, Pidal's work was 'una magnífica lección de patriotismo', while Ramón Pérez de Ayala described it as 'el libro más importante que se ha publicado en España hace mucho tiempo [...]; todo español ganoso de conciencia hispánica debiera leerlo y releerlo' (Lacarra 1980: 107). An editorial in the newspaper *El Debate* called the work 'una gran obra patriótica' (Pérez Villanueva 1991: 316). While there were some dissenting voices, notably that of José Ortega y Gasset (Pérez Pascual 1998: 211–12), they were drowned out by a general chorus of acclamation that spread well beyond the universities and learned societies of the day. María Eugenia Lacarra has demonstrated the strong impact that *La España del Cid* had in Spanish military circles too and the extent to which the ideas Menéndez Pidal had articulated so powerfully and persuasively were in turn appropriated by the propagandists of the Francoist Nationalist movement during and after the Spanish Civil War (Lacarra 1980).

Menéndez Pidal's conduct during the Civil War and its aftermath has given rise to considerable debate (Pérez Villanueva 1991: 381–8; Linehan 1996; Pérez Pascual 1998: 285–312; García Isasti 2004: 602–8). Yet the fact that his ideas were so enthusiastically adopted by the Nationalists — to the extent that General Franco was portrayed by his propagandists as a new *caudillo*, like the Cid rebelling against the constituted authority, but for the greater good — did not in turn mean that Menéndez Pidal was wholeheartedly sympathetic to the regime or that he was an 'ideólogo liberal del franquismo', as Lacarra has suggested (113). On the contrary, Menéndez Pidal's declaration of support for the Republic at the beginning of the hostilities, his long period of exile from Spain thereafter, and his perceived 'passivity' during the course of the war were viewed with considerable suspicion by the Francoist authorities and it was for that very reason that on his return from exile in Paris in 1939 he was stripped of the directorship of the Real Academia Española, required to appear before the 'Tribunal de Responsibilidades Políticas' as a suspected dissident, and for a time had his bank accounts frozen.

Los españoles en la historia

The year 1947 marked an important turning-point in Menéndez Pidal's fortunes. That year saw him restored to the directorship of the Real Academia, a post that he would hold uninterruptedly until his death. It also saw the publication of his long essay *Los españoles en la historia. Cimas y depresiones en la curva de su vida política*, which appeared as the prologue to the first volume of the collaborative *Historia de España*, published by Espasa Calpe, of which Menéndez Pidal was the founding editor. *Los españoles en la historia* was aimed at a Spanish population still traumatised by the events of the Civil War that had only recently concluded. The piece was by no means a work of traditional historical research, grounded upon painstaking analysis of a wide array of primary sources, in the way that *La España del Cid* most avowedly was. It was, rather, an extended essay in cultural history, a discursive meditation on Spain's historical development across more than two thousand years and, more to the point, on what Menéndez Pidal regarded as the eternal characteristics of the Spaniards themselves. In *Los españoles en la historia* Menéndez Pidal's longstanding preoccupation with the unity of Spain and what he regarded as a lack of sufficient *cohesión social* and *solidaridad cultural* among his countrymen would find full voice.

The essay is divided into five sections. In the first three, Menéndez Pidal sought to identify and explain what he saw as the essential and enduring traits of Spanishness across the ages, namely, *sobriedad, idealidad* and *individualismo*. In the fourth section, *Unitarismo y regionalismo*, he explored the very concept of Spain and the tensions that had existed between centre and periphery throughout Spanish history. The essay concludes with *Las dos Españas* — a conscious echo of Mariano José de Larra's mordant essay *El día de difuntos de 1836* — in which Menéndez Pidal pondered the ideological issues that had served to divide Spaniards in the past, as he put it, 'quebrantando la unidad moral de la colectividad' (lxxi). In the course of the essay, Menéndez Pidal ranges far and wide in time and place, from Roman Hispania to the still-born experiment in federalism under the First Republic in 1873–4. His canvas is vast and his brushstrokes are correspondingly broad. He only timidly refers to more recent events, however, and to the Spanish Civil War only very obliquely. This is a historian treading with extreme caution.

For Menéndez Pidal, Spanish history had always been subject to two countervailing forces: on the one hand there was the natural, metaphysical unity of the Spanish nation, with Castile as its heart; on the other the congenital *insolidaridad* of the Spaniards themselves, which had frequently caused national unity to crumble. However, he was adamant that however much the *cohesión nacional* of the Spaniards had suffered across the centuries, be it as a consequence of what he called 'sentimiento localista' (li), 'una particular debilidad del espíritu asociativo en España' (li), or the opposed ideologies of traditionalists and Europeanizing innovators (lxxxi–xcix), the spirit of Hispanic unity had endured and would yet prevail. Menéndez Pidal concluded this final chapter, written barely eight years after the end of the Civil War, with this heartfelt appeal for reconciliation between the two Spains:

> ¿Cesará este siniestro empeño de suprimir al adversario? […] Suprimir al disidente, sofocar propósitos de vida creída mejor por otros hermanos, es un atentado contra el acierto […] No es una de las semiespañas enfrentadas la que habrá de prevalecer en partido único poniendo epitafio a la otra. No será una España de la derecha o de la izquierda; será la España total, anhelada por tantos, la que no amputa uno de sus brazos, la que aprovecha íntegramente todas sus capacidades [...] una España tradicional inquebrantable en su catolicismo [...] A su vez una España nueva, llena de espíritu de modernidad (xcix–c).

He continues in resolutely optimistic tone:

> El dolor de la España única y eterna [...] traerá la necesaria reintegración, a pesar de la tremenda borrasca de antagonismos que azota al mundo. La normalización de la vida exigirá, mañana mismo, ideas de convivencia [...] La comprensiva ecuanimidad hará posible y fructífero a los españoles el convivir sobre el suelo patrio, no unánimes […] pero si aunados en un anhelo común hispánico […] Confraternados en los grandes e inmediatos designios colectivos, concordados en instaurar la selección mas justiciera, sin acepción de partido, acortarán las depresiones e interrupciones en la curva historica de nuestro pueblo y acabarán al fin con tantos bandazos de la nave estatal, para tomar un rumbo seguro hacia los altos destinos nacionales (ci).

To a large extent, the historical vision of Spain being articulated here by Menéndez Pidal drew on ideas that he had already rehearsed in *La España del Cid* and in other publications before that. The watchwords enunciated are *reintegración, normalización, convivencia*. The appeal for social cohesion is there and the depiction of the *Reconquista* as a collective enterprise of national reunification, with Castile as its driving force, is again to the fore. Walter Starkie described *Los españoles en la historia* as 'a calm dispassionate analysis [...] written by a scientist and a humanist in a mood of detached enquiry', but in truth it is anything but that, particularly in its final pages (Menéndez Pidal 1950: 111). Menéndez Pidal was above all a conservative nationalist who wore his heart on his sleeve, a man whose belief in 'la España única y eterna' (ci) was at the very core of his belief system and whose profound concern for national unity lay at the heart of most of his writings. 'In Menéndez Pidal's methodology', notes Michael Gerli, 'history, philology, and patriotism merge, each representing distinct facets of the same prism. The first two disciplines work in concert as a means for revealing an even greater reality, whose origin can be found in the third, the patriotic side — namely the sense and destiny of Spanish culture' (Gerli 2001: 113).

It should, of course, be emphasised that in seeking to isolate and delineate the essence of Spanishness or to identify the 'collective soul' of the Spaniards Menéndez Pidal was treading a well-worn path. In the aftermath of the collapse of the Spanish empire in 1898, numerous intellectuals, including historians, had tried to make sense of Spain's ignominious fall from grace and had sought to rediscover those elements that might yet contribute to the country's regeneration. In so doing, they began to probe the very essence of the Spanish soul (Franco 1980; Barton 1993: 108–12). Ángel Ganivet's *Idearium español* (1896) and Rafael Altamira's *Psicología del pueblo español* (1902) were particularly influential texts in this regard. To borrow Gerald Brenan's memorable metaphor, it was if Spain itself had become a patient on the psychoanalyst's couch (Brenan 1953: 419). Menéndez Pidal's work on the Cid was also fully in tune with writers like Unamuno, Machado and Azorín, who had extolled the eternal virtues of Castile, 'the spiritual motor of all Hispanic life' (Gerli 2001: 118–20). What was novel in Menéndez Pidal's approach was his attempt to steer a course between the ultra-traditionalist defenders of *la España castiza* on the one hand and those who argued that Spain's salvation lay in innovation on the other. As Joaquín

Pérez Villanueva has observed, 'La España contemporánea, según Pidal, ofrece un proyecto de continuidad histórica que se basa en una tradición viva abierta al cambio' (Pérez Villanueva 1991: 402).

When Menéndez Pidal took up his pen to write *Los españoles en la historia*, nigh on half a century after the loss of empire, these questions had not diminished in their significance to Spanish scholars; on the contrary, Spain's tragic descent into civil war had made the quest to understand Spain and 'the Spanish Predicament' all the more pressing. Indeed, far from being a throwback to the past, Menéndez Pidal's essay was soon to be followed by critiques in similar vein, and on a far greater scale, by his disciples Américo Castro (1948) and Claudio Sánchez-Albornoz (1956). But Menéndez Pidal's call for dialogue and concord was by no means in tune with the spirit of the times. It was, in fact, as José Ignacio Pérez Pascual has observed, a highly risky line to take, 'en un momento en el que seguían soplando [...] vientos de ciega persecución y se deseaba presentar la imagen de una España monolítica, liberada de los desvíos de la democracia merced a una gloriosa "Cruzada" y sometida a una ideología totalitaria en la que encuentran acomodo las corrientes más reaccionarias del catolicismo' (Pérez Pascual 1998: 313). Although many intellectuals gave Menéndez Pidal's essay a warm welcome (Pérez Villanueva 1991: 404–5), there were others, like Rafael Calvo Serer, who were not won over by the call for reconciliation, insisting instead upon the need to preserve 'la homogeneidad lograda en 1939' through the 'eliminación de discrepancias' (Pérez Pascual 1998: 314). Be that as it may, *Los españoles en la historia*, which was later reprinted, proved to be a best seller with the Spanish public and remained an immensely influential work for decades to come.

El Padre Las Casas

When Menéndez Pidal wrote *Los españoles en la historia* he was already well advanced in years, yet his historical endeavours were far from over. In 1963, at the ripe old age of 94, he published his last major book, *El Padre Las Casas: su doble personalidad*. In this polemical work he sought to discredit the so-called *Leyenda Negra* — which portrayed the Spanish settlement of the New World as a prolonged act of cruelty and rapacity rather than of civilization — by discrediting the career and writings of the most prominent and vocal critic of Spanish settlement in the Americas, Bartolomé de Las Casas. According to Menéndez Pidal, Las Casas was not merely misguided in his criticisms of the Spanish treatment of the Amerindian peoples, he was a paranoid schizophrenic. In the course of his study, he subjected Las Casas to a furious attack, denouncing variously his subject's 'anormalidad enfermiza' (xiv), 'interpretación paranoide' (13), 'infantil jactancia' (34), 'delirio de grandeza' (36), and 'dolencia mental' (312), to name but a few of the most grievous charges he levelled at the Dominican friar. Thus, Las Casas's decision to give up his encomienda of Indians in Hispaniola in 1514 marked 'el afloramiento de la enfermedad' (13–14). For Menéndez Pidal, Las Casas and the vainglorious and utterly deluded don Quixote were two of a kind: 'ufanos, orgullosos, muy llenos de sí [...] arrogantes' (337). In short, the work is the most sustained, vituperative piece of *ad hominem* polemic that you could possibly wish to see. It is, as Hess has remarked, 'a book that is often disturbing in its intransigence' (85). And it seems that Menéndez Pidal later regretted his intemperate attack. In 1965, in a conversation with Rafael Lapesa, then just back from a conference in England, don Ramón confided, 'Diga a los hispanistas ingleses que si volviera a escribir el libro sobre Las Casas, lo haría menos polémico' (Pérez Pascual 1998: 364). Although a few scholars responded positively to *El Padre Las Casas* and the patriotic tone of the work aroused a positive reaction in official circles, where it was doubtless seen as a boost to Spain's reputation in the world, the dominant reaction in the international academic community was a mixture of astonishment and embarrassment. While *La España del Cid* continued to be regarded, both in Spain and abroad, as a key work of historical scholarship on the eleventh century, it is probably no exaggeration to say that Menéndez Pidal's study of Las Casas sank pretty much without trace.[2]

---

[2]Equally controversial was Menéndez Pidal's essay 'El Compromiso de Caspe, autodeterminación de un pueblo' (1964), in which he argued that the dynastic agreement between Castile and Aragon in 1412, known as the 'Compromiso de Caspe', had been a positive step towards the creation, or rather reunification, of the Spanish state and that for the most part it had been enthusiastically supported by the Catalans themselves. The response in the Catalan academic establishment was frosty to say the least (Hess 1982: 76–7).

The Pidalian Legacy
Writing in 1960, José Antonio Maravall observed

> Hemos de reconocer que a Menéndez Pidal le debemos hoy los españoles, entre otras cosas, sencillamente, una nueva Historia de España […] (gracias al) gran maestro, se pondría en claro ante las gentes una línea histórica española dotada de sentido y capaz, a su vez, de darlo a los programas de futuro que los españoles, o por lo menos aquellos españoles necesitados de un esquema intelectualmente válido para organizar su existencia, formularan (Maravall 1960: 150–1).

At the beginning of the twenty-first century, there can be no doubt that Menéndez Pidal remains 'an intellectual and cultural institution, whose monumental corpus still cannot be approached without a certain amount of awe' (Brown 1995: 16; Gómez Moreno 2005); 'his name evokes instant recognition, veneration, and tones of hushed reverence [...]   He was and is still a legend whose vast oeuvre has endowed our sense of things Spanish with a certain lingering legendary quality' (Gerli 2001: 112). Be that as it may, it is probably fair to say that as a historian, at least, the figure of Menéndez Pidal does not cast quite the long shadow that it once did.   He retains a totemic status as one of the great scholars of Spanish history, certainly, but increasingly in the way in which British historians look back with respect at the work of, say, Maitland, Stubbs or Trevelyan, but use them or cite them only rarely.   As post-Francoist Spain has matured into a prosperous, self-confident society, fully integrated into the community of western democratic nations, historians no longer seem anxious, like the intellectuals of the 'Generation of '98' and their successors, to find a solution to 'the Spanish Predicament' or to identify the characteristics that make up Spain's *Volksgeist*. The devolution of powers from the centre to the regions through a regime of *comunidades autonómas* has given rise to a powerful shift in attitudes and perspectives at all levels of society, not least in the academic profession. Accordingly, Pidalian concerns to nurture the *alma colectiva* of the nation and his vision of the *Reconquista* as a shared national enterprise, with Castile as the driving force in national reunification, have fallen decidedly out of fashion. Instead, influenced in particular by the approaches of the French *Annales* school, scholarly emphasis has been upon diversity rather than unity, upon the importance of socio-economic forces rather than the power of ideas. True, the figure of the Cid continues to keep numerous academics in gainful employment and is the subject of umpteen publications and conferences, as well as a children's cartoon and even a rock song, but he is no longer invoked by politicians and intellectuals as a role model for twenty-first century Spaniards to follow and emulate, and to my knowledge *La España del Cid* is no longer required reading for Spanish military cadets. Instead, the patriotic vision of the Cid that Menéndez Pidal penned has come under sustained academic attack. As Richard Fletcher has observed, 'His famous book still stands, though now with somewhat the air of a medieval castle under siege' (Fletcher 1989: 205). The debate over the essence of Spanishness, pursued with such vigour and at such length by Menéndez Pidal and others, no longer dominates the academic agenda, even if the question of the unity of Spain and the 'dos Españas' remains a hot topic for politicians and intellectuals alike.

Yet even if the name of Menéndez Pidal is not now invoked so religiously or reverently as once used to be the case, the arguments he articulated so forcefully are by no means moribund. A recent biography of the Cid by Gonzalo Martínez Diez (1999), which places particular emphasis on the unswerving loyalty of the Castilian warlord to Alfonso VI, is strikingly Pidalian in some of its intellectual and philosophical viewpoints. Even if the author eschews what he calls the outright *cidofilia* of Menéndez Pidal, he is none the less keen to reject what he calls 'ciertas descalificaciones de nuestros días que sólo proceden del rencor, de la ignorancia y de la incapacidad de comprender cierta clase de valores' (15). Also worthy of mention is Miguel Ángel Ladero Quesada's *La formación medieval de España. Territorios. Regiones. Reinos* (2004), which is by no means a throwback to the past, but rather a sober and concise reassessment of the complex process of territorial expansion by which the Christian states of northern Iberia extended their control over the entire peninsula between the eighth and the fifteenth centuries. But there is a political message too. Like a latter-day Menéndez Pidal, Ladero issues a warning to those who would deny that Spain, or at any rate the concept of Spain, did indeed exist during the Middle Ages. To do so, he claims, is to distort the history of the Peninsula. If contemporaries can only grasp this fact, Ladero contends, 'se puede imaginar un futuro mejor para todos' (57). Who is to say that at some point in the future, in the renewed search for *cohesión social* or *solidaridad nacional*, the collective memory of the Cid and the *Reconquista*, so lovingly and passionately articulated by Menéndez Pidal, will not be dusted down by his fellow Spaniards and pressed into service once more?

Works Cited

ALTAMIRA, Rafael, 1902. *Psicología del pueblo español* (Barcelona: Minerva).

BARTON, Simon, 1993. 'The Roots of the National Question in Spain', in *The National Question in Europe in Historical Context*, eds. Mikuláš Teich and Roy Porter (Cambridge: UP), 106–27.

BRENAN, Gerald, 1953. *The Literature of the Spanish People: From Roman Times to the Present Day*, 2nd edn (Cambridge: UP).

BROWN, Catherine, 1995. 'The Relics of Menéndez Pidal: Mourning and Melancholia in Hispanomedieval Studies', *C*, 24, 15–41.

CASTRO, Américo, 1948. *España en su historia: cristianos, moros y judíos* (Buenos Aires: Editorial Losada).

DOZY, Reinhart, 1849. *Recherches sur l'histoire et la littérature de l'Espagne pendant le moyen âge*, 2 vols, 2nd and 3rd eds, 1860 and 1881 (Leiden: E. J. Brill).

FLETCHER, Richard, 1989. *The Quest for El Cid* (London: Weidenfeld & Nicolson).

FRANCO, Dolores, 1980. *España como preocupación. Antología* (Barcelona: Argos Vegara).

GANIVET, Ángel, 1896. *Idearium español*, 11th edn, 1981 (Madrid: Espasa-Calpe).

GARCÍA ISASTI, Prudencio, 2004. *La España metafísica. Lectura crítica del pensamiento de Ramón Menéndez Pidal (1891–1936)* (Bilbao: Real Academia de la Lengua Vasca/Euskaltzaindia).

GERLI, E. Michael, 2001. 'Inventing the Spanish Middle Ages: Ramón Menéndez Pidal, Spanish Cultural History, and Ideology in Philology', *C*, 30, 111–26.

GÓMEZ MORENO, Ángel, 2005. 'Ramón Menéndez Pidal (1869–1968)', in *Rewriting the Middle Ages in the Twentieth Century*, eds. Jaume Aurell and Francisco Crosas (Turnhout: Brepols), 69–85.

HESS, Steven, 1982. *Ramón Menéndez Pidal* (Boston: Twayne Publishers).

LACARRA, María Eugenia, 1980. 'La utilización del Cid de Menéndez Pidal en la ideología militar franquista', *Ideologies and Literature* 3, 95–127.

LADERO QUESADA, Miguel Ángel, 2004. *La formación medieval de España. Territorios. Regiones. Reinos* (Madrid: Alianza Editorial).

LINEHAN, Peter, 1993. *History and the Historians of Medieval Spain* (Oxford: Clarendon Press).

——, 1996. 'The Court Historiographer of Francoism? La Leyenda oscura of Ramón Menéndez Pidal', *BHS* (Glasgow) 73 (1996), 437–50.

Maravall, José Antonio, 1960. *Menéndez Pidal y la historia del pensamiento* (Madrid: Arión).

Martínez Diez, Gonzalo, 1999. *El Cid histórico* (Barcelona: Editorial Planeta).

Masdeu, Juan Francisco, 1783–1805. *Historia crítica de España y de la cultura española*, 20 vols (Madrid: Imprenta de Sancha).

Menéndez Pidal, Ramón, 1896. *La leyenda de los Infantes de Lara* (Madrid: Imprenta de Hijos de J. M. Ducazcal).

——, 1906. *Primera crónica general. Estoria de España que mandó componer Alfonso el Sabio y se continuaba bajo Sancho IV en 1289* (Madrid: Bailly-Baillière); 2nd edn, 2 vols (Madrid: Gredos, 1955); 3rd edn, ed. Diego Catalán, 2 vols (Madrid: Fundación Menéndez Pidal/Universidad Autónoma de Madrid, 1977).

——, 1908–11. *Cantar de Mio Cid: texto, gramática y vocabulario* (Madrid: Bailly-Baillière).

——, 1921. *El Cid en la historia* (Madrid: Jiménez y Molina).

——, 1929. *La España del Cid*, 2 vols., 7th ed. 1969 (Madrid: Espasa-Calpe).

——, 1940. *Idea imperial de Carlos V* (Madrid: Espasa-Calpe).

——, 1947. 'Los españoles en la historia: cimas y depresiones en la curva de su vida política', prologue to *Historia de España*, vol. I, (Madrid: Espasa Calpe), viii–ciii.

——, 1950. *El imperio hispánico y los cinco reinos. Dos épocas en la estructura política de España* (Madrid: Instituto de Estudios Políticos).

——, 1950. *The Spaniards in Their History*. Translated with a Prefatory Essay by Walter Starkie (London: Hollis Carter).

——, 1963. *El Padre Las Casas: su doble personalidad* (Madrid: Espasa-Calpe).

——, 1964. 'El Compromiso de Caspe, autodeterminación de un pueblo', prologue to *Historia de España*, vol. XV (Madrid: Espasa-Calpe), ix–clxvi.

Pérez Pascual, José Ignacio, 1998. *Ramón Menéndez Pidal. Ciencia y pasión* (Valladolid: Junta de Castilla y León).

Pérez Villanueva, Joaquín, 1991. *Ramón Menéndez Pidal. Su vida y su tiempo* (Madrid: Espasa-Calpe).

Sánchez-Albornoz, Claudio, 1956. *España: un enigma histórico*, 2 vols (Buenos Aires: Editorial Sudamericana).

Menéndez Pidal and the Beginnings of Ibero-Romance Dialectology: A Critical Survey One Century Later[1]

INÉS FERNÁNDEZ-ORDÓÑEZ

(*Universidad Autónoma de Madrid*)

When Ramón Menéndez Pidal began his intellectual activity at the start of the last century, little or nothing had been done to incorporate the theoretical principles and methods developed by European philologists at the end of the nineteenth century into the sphere of Spanish linguistics. Some forty years later, however, when the Civil War interrupted the research projects of Menéndez Pidal and his colleagues, shutting down the Centro de Estudios Históricos and forcing the researchers to disperse or go into exile, Hispanic philology had come into existence, and was largely comparable with the philology of other European countries.

   It was in the first few years of the twentieth century that the serious study of Spanish dialects began, under the leadership of Menéndez Pidal. The start of Spanish dialectology was not accidental, nor the result of a short-lived interest, but part of a long-term plan that he had developed. As early as 1903, he wrote a letter to Miguel de Unamuno mentioning his interest in studying the Leonese and Aragonese dialects and writing two monographs about them:

> Mi ambición es hacer dos libritos, uno sobre el Leonés y otro sobre el Aragonés, que sean la base para una futura historia de la Lengua española que algún día escribiré. Sé que la tarea es muy grande, pues tengo que perderme primero en pormenores y luego organizar conjuntos; pero si tengo vida, espero realizar mi idea.[2]

The planned monograph on Leonese, *El dialecto leonés*, was published in 1906; but the one he had planned to dedicate to Aragonese was never completed, in spite of the fact that the first two studies he

---

[1] I owe the English version of this paper to Roger Wright's kind generosity.
[2] Quoted by Catalán (2005: 89) and Pérez Pascual (1998: 81).

made of texts containing dialect data, the *Poema de Yusuf* (1902) and the *Razón de amor* (1905), were dedicated to texts showing Aragonese features. I will not expand here on the reasons for the postponement of the Aragonese monograph, which might have been academic, political or personal.[3]   *El dialecto leonés* was undoubtedly the first monograph that systematically organized all the linguistic data available at that time for an Ibero-Romance dialect area, so it can be seen as the symbol of the start of the research into Ibero-Romance dialects carried out by Menéndez Pidal and his colleagues.

But *El dialecto leonés* is far from being an isolated achievement. It needs to be seen in the context of Menéndez Pidal's other publications (section I below), and those inspired and supported by him in the Centro de Estudios Históricos (section II).

I. The first dialect studies

Poema de Yuçuf. Materiales para su estudio (1902)
Manual de gramática histórica española (1904)
Razón de amor con los Denuestos del agua y el vino (1905)
El dialecto leonés (1906)
Cantar de Mio Cid. Texto, gramática y vocabulario (1908–11)
Elena y María. Poesía leonesa inédita del siglo XIII (1914)
Review of A. Griera i Gaja, *La frontera catalano-aragonesa* (1916)
Roncesvalles. Un nuevo cantar de gesta español del siglo XIII (1917)

---

[3]Academic reasons could have included the fact that Umphrey published an article on Aragonese in 1911 which Menéndez Pidal referred to as a reliable description of the characteristics of Old Aragonese (1923: 19). His plan to write a monograph on Aragonese must have lasted until at least 1906, when he addressed the first *Congrés de la Llengua Catalana* on the border between Aragonese and Valencian (Fernández-Ordóñez 2006: 174–75). A possible political reason could have been the controversy which accompanied his article 'Cataluña bilingüe' in 1902, in which he discussed whether Castilian in Catalonia was a foreign import or had been present for centuries (Cid 1991: 539–49, esp. 541–42; Pérez Pascual 1998: 79–80; Perea 2005: 263–78, 287–92; García Isasti 2004: 336–42; Morgades 2006: 33–38). A personal reason could have been that Aragonese never interested him as much as Asturian. Given the origin of his family, as well as his childhood journeys to Asturias, it is likely that he did not have as much first-hand data on Aragonese as he had on Asturian (Pérez Villanueva 1991: 23–37). The many surveys which he planned and carried out after 1906, in 1907, 1910, 1912, 1932 and from 1946 to 50, when he was aiming to improve his knowledge of the Asturian linguistic domain (Catalán & Galmés 1989: 167–70), reveal that he was always attracted more to Asturian than to Aragonese.

Documentos lingüísticos de España. Reino de Castilla (1919)
Orígenes del español (1926)

II. Collections of dialect data inspired by Menéndez Pidal

Tomás Navarro Tomás (dir.), *Atlas lingüístico de la Península Ibérica* (1923–36)
Tomás Navarro Tomás, *Documentos lingüísticos del Alto Aragón* (1919)
Américo Castro and Federico de Onís, *Fueros leoneses de Zamora, Salamanca, Ledesma y Alba de Tormes* (1916)
By 1936, these studies had established the basic pattern of the dialects spoken on the Iberian Peninsula; both those spoken in the present, as the *Atlas Lingüístico de la Península Ibérica* compiled the twentieth century data, and in the past, as the publication of medieval documents and texts made it possible to know their remote medieval origins.

The research methodology used by Menéndez Pidal in the studies mentioned in section I remained largely the same in all of them, from 1900 until the Civil War, and subsequently in his later studies. All his publications show some consistent features in their working methods; that is, his conclusions are always reached in accordance with certain recurring techniques (section III):

III. Methodology

1. The interpretation of medieval data is combined with, and supported by, present-day findings; and vice versa. This can be observed in *El dialecto leonés*, *Manual de gramática histórica*, *Cantar de Mio Cid* and *Orígenes del español*.

2. More is required than just combining medieval and current data. It is necessary to gather data from every Romance dialect spoken on the Iberian Peninsula. Linguistic phenomena are interpreted by comparing the data found on the peninsula; in particular, Castilian can be understood only by comparing it with the Leonese and Aragonese dialects.

3. Evidence from toponymy is valuable in addition to the modern and ancient data; toponymy is considered to be of particular relevance when testing the validity of proposed hypotheses.

4. The vast majority of the data discussed are of a phonetic nature. Historical phonetics is the architectural framework, to which Menéndez Pidal adds grammatical and lexical support.

5. For Menéndez Pidal it was not enough just to establish the territorial distribution of linguistic phenomena. He aimed to discover the historical reasons for the formation of each linguistic area, and for the linguistic preferences of each human community. His need to find the effective historical cause for each phenomenon has a corollary: according to Menéndez Pidal, linguistic evidence is of equal, if not greater, importance than written records for reconstructing the history of a given place or area; that is, linguistics is a branch of general history.

6. In addition, we can already see in *Orígenes del español* the 'diffusion' hypothesis of linguistic change. This implies that the more frequent and more consistent the data are for the occurrence of a linguistic phenomenon, the older it is. From a methodological point of view, this hypothesis is based on statistics (e.g. concerning the evolution of the diphthong *ai*, of the *m'n* combination, or of forms derived from *medietate*) and on comparisons between different peninsular geographical areas (the geographical-chronological criterion) which allow one to identify the focal area of the spread of these linguistic phenomena. The importance of using statistics as a means to reach conclusions reappears from time to time in his later works; for example, in the *Historia de la lengua española* written in exile during and after the Civil War, and published posthumously in 2005.[4]

This methodology is used in support of his views about the linguistic organization of the Iberian Peninsula, which can be summarised as two fundamental ideas: the first is the overwhelming role that Castilian played in the development of the Spanish language; the second is that the Spanish language is the result of the evolution of the Peninsula's three central Romance dialects: Castilian, Astur-Leonese and Navarro-Aragonese.

IV. Castilian's leading role in the development of Spanish

Menéndez Pidal's best known view is his consistent claim that Castile played a fundamental role in the development of the Spanish language. This idea has two sources. On one hand, it corresponds to the desire of the Generation of 1898 to restore the prosperity of the Spanish nation; in the same way as Azorín and Unamuno did,

---

[4]See, for example, the discussion of final vowel apocope (2005: 547–53, 580–84 & 643–44); of *leísmo* (2005: 1019–24); or of the aspiration of Latin F-(2005: 999–1003).

Menéndez Pidal ascribed to Castile a leading role in the shaping of Spain. On the other hand — this is what I consider to be the deciding factor for Menéndez Pidal — Castile had achieved that leading role because of a cultural factor: the attractiveness of its literature.[5]

According to Menéndez Pidal, Castilian was the first language to have its own literature. It was the language of epic poetry, and that literature exerted such a powerful attraction that it made Castilian the language of literature par excellence:

> Esos poemas tradicionales de Castilla, renovados por la actividad y la erudición de los juglares, eran literatura oral, efímera: el único cantar de gesta cuyo manuscrito se nos conservó, el de *Mio Cid*, no es castellano. Los cantares épicos castellanos no consiguieron perpetuarse en las bibliotecas, pero su popularidad los imponía a la atención del cronista autor de la Najerense, y *ellos, sobre toda otra producción literaria, ganaban crédito y admiración para el dialecto castellano.* (My italics; Menéndez Pidal 2005: 472)

This is why Menéndez Pidal was irritated by the evidence of the first literary texts, which were not always written in Castilian. So even though he acknowledged that in *Razón de amor* 'aragonés, como el copista, es el lenguaje del texto', he refused to accept that the author was Aragonese too: 'no podemos asegurar si el aragonesismo de este texto es propio del autor, o sólo del copista Lope [...]. El estar el pueblo de Moros a unas cinco leguas de la frontera occidental aragonesa, pudiera apoyar la suposición de un original poético venido de Castilla' (1905: 108–09).

This attitude can also be found in his analysis of *Elena y María*. The fact that the language of this poem did not attest the regularity which he expected to find in the articulation of diphthongs — as usual his line of argument was based upon a phonetic feature — was used to undermine the importance of Leonese as a language of literature, even though he accepted that the *Poema de Mio Cid* attests similar inconsistencies:

> Los textos literarios y los diplomas notariales [leoneses] no concuerdan en su testimonio; ni aquellos ni estos reflejan con suficiente fidelidad el dialecto leonés hablado; y en los textos

---

[5] See Portolés (1986), Armistead (2001), Gerli (2001), Santano (2003), Garatea Grau (2005) and the much less thorough analysis by García Isasti (2004).

> literarios, especialmente, se ven luchar dos influencias, lite-
> rarias también, y enteramente opuestas, la galaico-portuguesa
> y la castellana, que no se ejercieron de igual modo, ni mucho
> menos en la lengua hablada. La lengua hablada mantuvo
> hasta hoy caracteres propios bien armonizados entre sí, en
> los cuales se observa la transición gradual en el espacio, de
> los rasgos gallego-portugueses hasta los castellanos; en vez
> de esta transición gradual, los textos escritos nos muestran
> mezcla antagónica, pues la literatura leonesa, falta de perso-
> nalidad, se movió vacilante entre los dos centros de atención
> que incontrastablemente la sobrepujaban. (1914: 156)[6]

But of all the non-Castilian texts of the thirteenth century which did not conform to Menéndez Pidal's view of the dominance of Castilian language and literature, it was the *Roncesvalles* fragment which particularly worried him. While the *Poema de Mio Cid* more or less fits his theory that epic poetry had its origins in Castile (he located its first manifestation in the *Infantes de Lara*), the only other epic poem to be preserved was copied down in the Navarrese dialect. As a result, he insisted on snatching it away from Navarre and granting it to Castile:

> En resumen, diremos que las formas navarro-aragonesas que
> ofrece nuestro texto son muy pocas, muchas menos aún que

----

[6]For the whole question of the medieval representation of diphthongs in the Leonese area it is now worth consulting the new analysis made by Pascual (2004), and the observations of Wright (2000) in his comparative analysis of the spelling options chosen in the Leonese and Castilian versions of the Tratado de Cabreros of 1206. It seems to be clear that the rarity of written representations of rising diphthongs in León may have something to do with the presence of less regular diphthongizations in León than Menéndez Pidal envisaged, or with scribal traditions different from those of Castile; but either way we cannot conclude, as Menéndez Pidal did, that those written traditions had as a result 'menos personalidad'. Pascual (2004: 518–24) points out that in the twelfth-century documents from León the difficulties which they experienced in representing rising diphthongs were not felt when representing the monophthongization of falling diphthongs: the result is that, depending on the feature which we are concentrating on, Leonese scribal traditions can appear to be either relatively conservative or as innovative as those of Castile. Wright (2000: 79–82), for his part, points out that the Leonese chancery's version of the Tratado de Cabreros finds it easier than the Castilian version to represent the diphthong *ie* (except in the future subjunctive) and that both versions alternate in roughly the same proportions between the use in writing of *o* or *ue*. All these are facts which cast some doubt on the phonetic and graphic decisions ascribed by Menéndez Pidal to Castilian.

las que ocurren en los documentos del sur de Navarra (Fitero, Tudela) [...]. De modo que nuestro manuscrito presenta un desequilibrio entre la grafía y las formas dialectales; su carácter navarro se debe, pues, en gran parte a un amanuense, y acaso a éste se le puedan atribuir no sólo en gran parte, sino en su totalidad los dialectalismos navarros [...]. El lugar en que se redactó el poema de *Roncesvalles* pudiera ser Navarra. Cierto que no nos lo asegura ningún navarrismo de rima que se halle en nuestro fragmento; mas acaso parecerá natural que Navarra, el país que primero recibía a los juglares franceses que pasaban por el puerto de Roncesvalles a Santiago y otros puntos, se interesase primero por una leyenda que se desarrollaba en su propio territorio [...]. No obstante, [...] como se desconoce una literatura poética navarra en general, como se desconocen hasta meros relatos en prosa navarra acerca de la leyenda de Roncesvalles, y, por otra parte, como la literatura épica es muy activa en Castilla, como en ésta el desastre de Carlomagno fue popular hasta dar nacimiento a otro tema, el de Bernardo del Carpio, y como, en fin, la métrica de *Roncesvalles* es en extremo parecida a la de *Mio Cid*, parece más natural suponer que en Castilla se compuso el *Roncesvalles*, y que el lenguaje navarro con que hoy se nos presenta el fragmento recién descubierto es fruto simplemente de una adaptación debida a cualquier copista. (1917: 23 & 90)

Roncesvalles made it necessary to consider the possibility of Navarrese epic literature. Equally influenced by Navarre was Castilian Extremadura, where the *Poema de Mio Cid* was supposed to have been composed. Also Navarrese was the *Crónica najerense* written towards the end of the twelfth century, which contained the first summaries, in Latin prose, of many of the epic songs that had been lost in their original verse form. Nevertheless, Menéndez Pidal believed that the topics of the poems incorporated in the *Crónica najerense* must have been Castilian.[7]

The first written literary evidence was not composed in Castilian.

---

[7]'La *Crónica Najerense*, escrita a raíz de la muerte del emperador Alfonso VII, hacia 1160, nos da resumen o prosificación latina de cinco poemas de asunto castellano' (2005: 471). This is a highly debatable statement, since several of the poems could easily be considered to be Navarrese or Aragonese, including, for instance, the story of the succession of Sancho el Mayor. Rather than containing specifically Castilian topics, what the stories collected in the chronicle seem to share is a distaste for the Kingdom of León.

But Menéndez Pidal had no hesitation in uprooting it from its origins, classifying that literature as 'dialectal' in his *Historia de la lengua*. Calling it 'dialectal' only makes sense, of course, from an anachronistic Castilian nationalist perspective in which Castilian has already been identified as the variety which would later prevail as the language of literature.[8] However, if we consider that one of the fundamental steps in initiating the standardization process of a linguistic variety is the formation of a written representation for it, it could be argued that in this early period, due to the absence of Castilian written literature, it is Castilian which should be considered as being 'dialectal', as compared with, for example, Navarro-Aragonese, which is attested in such works as the *Razón de amor* and the *Liber regum*.

At the heart of Menéndez Pidal's linguistic Castilian nationalism there lay a literary nationalism. Its origin lay in his view that traditional poetry is the only genuine expression of the collective soul of the Spanish people. This idea can be seen clearly be in the quotation below, in which the first written works of literature are not taken entirely seriously, on the grounds that they are 'dialectal' and imitations of foreign models, while on the other hand the literature of the oral tradition, whose origin and linguistic expression is considered to be Castilian, is highly praised, despite only being attested indirectly in the sources:

> Castilla, durante el reinado de Alfonso VIII, afirma más que
> en los períodos anteriores su individualidad lingüística y
> propaga rápidamente su influencia por los dialectos circun-
> vecinos. *No se conserva en este tiempo obra ninguna en castellano
> que nos revele gran actividad poética o prosística como apoyo de la
> preponderancia idiomática.* [...] Mientras la literatura escrita,
> de imitación de modelos foráneos, escrita en pareados o en
> cuaderna vía, continúa firme en su dialectalismo, los juglares

---

[8]Chapter X of part III is entitled 'Esplendor de la literatura dialectal (1140–1180)'; section 8 is called 'Carácter dialectal de la literatura'. In chapter XI, the titles of section 1, 'Preponderancia castellana', and section 7, 'Castellanización de la lengua literaria', contrast with those of section 6 'Convivencia y mixtura de dialectos' and section 8 'Dialectalismo cancilleresco y notarial'. In chapter II of part IV, which discusses the language of the *Mester de Clerecía*, section 1 is entitled 'Dialectalismo atenuado'. In all of these sections, every linguistic form which is not Castilian is described as 'dialectal'. Castilian Extremadura and the Kingdom of Toledo are among the areas considered to be non-Castilian; this is why the *Auto de los reyes magos* and the *Poema de Mio Cid* are not considered to be Castilian.

castellanos conseguían para Castilla la hegemonía de la literatura cuasi-oral. (My italics; Menéndez Pidal 2005: 474–75)

It is well known that Menéndez Pidal took it as axiomatic that the
romancero could be found 'wherever Spanish is spoken', and the
fact that the language of the ballads sung in Galicia or Catalonia
is Castilian, proved, as he understood it, the vitality of Castilian
literature, and also of the language in which that literature was transmitted.[9] This argument was constantly used to argue that Spanish
had been spoken for many centuries in Catalonia, which explains
why Catalan folklorists have reacted by showing little interest in their
own *romancero*.[10]

The successful expansion of the Castilian language is, according
to Menéndez Pidal, a result of its irresistible literature.[11] Castilian
poetry is revolutionary, and so, in the same way, the language
that conveys it must also be revolutionary. The dissident, deviant,
rebellious and innovative characteristics of Castilian are constantly
repeated in *Orígenes del español*, as in these two brief extracts:

> Se ve que la tendencia vulgar a suprimir la *g-* estuvo algo
> extendida por casi toda España, aunque sólo en la revolu-
> cionaria Castilla arraigó decididamente. (1950: 235)

---

[9]Thus, when commenting on the ballad written down by the Majorcan Jaume
de Olesa in 1421, the first preserved documentation of a 'lyrical' ballad, he
said: 'el castellano, en sus manifestaciones populares, hablado o cantado, ejerce
influjo poético en tierra catalana antes e independientemente de su difusión
política. La lengua no sigue al imperio, como decía Nebrija; la lengua sigue a la
cultura' (2005: 647).

[10]'Muchos folkloristas catalanes dejaron de interesarse por *su* romancero, excelente
como pura poesía sin más, al recelar que no fuera tan netamente catalán como
deseaban' (Cid 1991: 550). Nevertheless, there are bilingual areas which have not
accepted the *romancero* as a genre of oral transmission; for example, the Basque
Country, despite using Romance for many centuries and the intensive contact
it has had with Castile (Cid 1991). On the other hand, contrary to Menéndez
Pidal's assumption, in Catalonia, Galicia and Portugal the ballads display a hybrid
linguistic nature, or even complete adaptation to the language of the area; see the
studies carried out by Forneiro on the languages used in the Galician *romancero*
(2000, 2004, 2005, 2010).

[11]Garatea Grau (2005) accurately highlights the parallel between his *tradicionalismo
literario*, the theory which he developed on the basis of his study of the ballads,
and its subsequent expansion into *tradicionalismo lingüístico*, which pervades his
conception of how linguistic changes operate: they begin in the speech of particular
individuals, and then acquire supporters until they are, or are not, accepted by the
community as a whole.

> El artículo en Castilla se encuentra más adelantado en su
> evolución [...]. Las grandes vacilaciones de forma que el
> artículo tiene en León y en Aragón son en Castilla poquísimo
> usadas o totalmente desconocidas. Castilla, como en otros
> fenómenos que ya hemos notado, es la región en que la
> evolución se ha realizado más rápida y decididamente. (1950:
> 337 & 339)

Such comments are reiterated throughout the book, and conclude
with his well-known summary of the revolutionary features found
in Castilian — apart from the article, they are all phonetic features —
and the following statement:

> Cantabria, la última conquista romana, y además comarca
> de romanización más lenta, nos aparece en su evolución
> lingüística como región más indócil a la común evolución de
> las otras regiones, más revolucionaria, más inventiva, original
> y dada al neologismo [...]. Hemos visto que Castilla aparece
> en la Historia rechazando el código visigótico vigente en toda
> la Península y desarrollando una legislación consuetudinaria
> local. Pues lo mismo sucede con el lenguaje. El dialecto
> castellano representa en todas esas características una nota
> diferencial frente a los demás dialectos de España, como una
> fuerza rebelde y discordante que surge de Cantabria y de las
> regiones circunvecinas. (1950: 487)

This reconstruction of the geographical area in which Castilian originated, as Cantabria and its surrounding areas, seems to me to be
essentially right, although some rephrasing of Menéndez Pidal's
statement is necessary. For a start, it is obvious that the terms
'archaic and conservative' and 'revolutionary and innovative' are
inappropriate when describing dialects; those attributes depend
mainly on which features are selected for analysis. There are some
instances in which the Castilian developments could be considered
to be the 'conservative' ones; examples would include the absence
of diphthongization before a yod, and the absence of palatalization
of initial L-. On the other hand, in the *Orígenes* Menéndez Pidal
never highlights the non-Castilian linguistic features which were
later preferred over Castilian ones in the formation of the common
Spanish language; an example of this is the form *mitad*, which was
established much earlier in the East (as he shows in the book; 1950[3]:
265–70). The same tendency has been observed in the discussion of

the assimilation of MB> *m*, which also had its origin in the East, or the palatalization of PL-, KL- and FL-, which originated in the West; in these examples Castile was an 'área intermedia, ni pionera ni radical' (Cano Aguilar 1998: 130).

Menéndez Pidal's desire to stress the revolutionary linguistic nature of Castilian created problems for him when texts which he regarded as Castilian because of their geographic location do not attest Castilian linguistic features. This is why, acknowledging the Navarro-Aragonese nature of the *Glosas Silenses*, he refrained from considering them to be Castilian, despite the geographical location which they belong to, and the scribal tradition which they were written in:

> Las Glosas Silenses, si por la escritura de su amanuense son tan castellanas como lo que se escribía por los monjes a las orillas del Arlanza, por su lenguaje son tan riojanas, casi, como lo que se escribía en las celdas de San Millán [...]. La falta de documentos notariales viejos de Silos nos impide comprobar el lenguaje de las Glosas Silenses. Es de suponer que todos estos rasgos navarro-riojanos que hemos apuntado no eran comunes a la alfoz de Lara, sino que eran lenguaje individual del monje glosador que quería seguir el patrón de los escritos usuales en el monasterio navarro de San Millán. (1950: 484–85)

Never let it be said that Navarrese had been infiltrating into the heart of Castile!

For similar reasons, he does not accept that the documents from Oña accurately reflect the local speech, supposedly as a result of archaism in their notarial traditions, even though in other areas, such as León, he takes such archaism as belonging to their speech:

> El idioma castellano que servía para la elocuencia de este conde Sancho García era una continuación progresada del idioma que había servido para redactar las Glosas Silenses en los tiempos ya lejanos de Fernán González [...]; pero no conocemos muestras de esa progresada habla vulgar castellana, sino sólo de su variedad latinizada que usaban los notarios. En el archivo del monasterio de Oña, fundado por el mismo Sancho García en 1011, y rico depósito de buena parte de nuestros documentos lingüísticos, todavía podemos descubrir algunos restos del habla vulgar corriente en el Norte del condado de Sancho, la cual conservaba fossateira, junto

> a la forma nueva más general, fossadera o 'fonsadera', y
> prefería aún lomba y portiello, canaliella, en vez de los neo-
> logismos loma, portillo, etc, que se usaban ya corrientemente
> en Castilla. (1950: 477)

In a similar way, because he was following a criterion for identifying
linguistic areas based *a priori* on political frontiers, Menéndez Pidal
sometimes collated evidence from Eastern León with that from the
rest of the Kingdom of León, thereby concealing the fact that the
original Castilian and Eastern Leonese features were the same. This
is what happened, for example, in the case of the evolution of words
that started with BR-, FR-, or the evolution of the *ai* diphthong,
in which the evidence from Sahagún matches that from Castile.[12]
Nevertheless, with regard to some other developments, such as those
of M'N, KT> *tf*, or SK^E> *ts*, Menéndez Pidal openly acknowledged that
the Eastern part of León coincided with Castilian; but even so, when
commenting on the data, he always emphasized that Castilian was
the leader:

> Una vez más Castilla sigue evolución diversa de la mayoría
> de los romances: *fascia > haça*. (1950[3]: 308)

> El neologismo de la *ch* en *pechar, lecho*, ya aludido, que se
> propaga por el Oriente y el Centro del reino astur-leonés,
> obedece probablemente a influjo castellano. Seguramente
> viene de Burgos el grupo *mbr* en vez de las formas leonesas
> *mn, m* en *nombre, techumbre*, etc. (1950[3]: 452)

It could be argued that this kind of distortion also applies to the
definite article, since in Eastern León the solutions coincided with
those of Castile much earlier than those of the rest of the Kingdom.[13]
As regards *leísmo* applied to masculine count nouns, there is also
the same usage in Eastern León and the original area of Castilian.[14]
Perhaps we should consider, then, whether this coincidence is also
original: if so, the early Castilian linguistic area should be expanded
westwards to include the Eastern part of the old Kingdom of León.

We know today that some of the allegedly differentiating Castilian
features had a much wider diffusion than that acknowledged by
Menéndez Pidal; for instance, the change from -LY-> ʒ and G^{E,I}->

---

[12]As Pascual and Santiago (2003) have shown.
[13]As can be deduced from Egido (2003).
[14]See Fernández-Ordóñez (1994, 2001, 2006–07) and Matute (2004).

Ø. Re-evaluation of the documents used by Menéndez Pidal has revealed much less consistent phenomena within Castilian than we are given to believe in the *Orígenes*.[15]

But all these observations are only of relatively minor importance. Menéndez Pidal's framework, and, in my view, his reconstruction of many of the linguistic details up to the eleventh century, are primarily correct, even though they could be improved, amended and refined with the help of new documents in more reliable editions. The main mistake, or rather one of the main mistakes, in the *Orígenes*, probably lies in Menéndez Pidal's conclusions at the end, where he assumes that the history of the Spanish language after the end of the eleventh century has been securely established; that is, he took the evolution of the language from the twelfth century onwards for granted, without basing it on the same firm foundations on which his interpretation of the language of the ninth to eleventh centuries was based. The least convincing part of the *Orígenes* consists of the following well-known words towards the end:

> Hasta el siglo XI los dialectos romances de la Península tenían distribución y relaciones muy diversas de las que estamos habituados a considerar más propias de ellos desde el siglo XIII acá. Los rasgos de los dos extremos dialectales que los diferencian del castellano, es decir, los rasgos del leonés y gallego al Occidente y los del aragonés y catalán al Oriente, no sólo se acercaban más por el Norte, estrechando en medio a los rasgos castellanos, sino que se unían por el Centro y por el Sur mediante el habla mozárabe de Toledo, de Badajoz, de Andalucía y de Valencia, análoga a la de los extremos en muchos de sus rasgos principales. Castilla no era más que un pequeño rincón donde fermentaba una disidencia lingüística muy original, pero que apenas ejercía cierta influencia expansiva.

The reconstruction can still be accepted up to this point, apart from his comments on *mozárabe*. But in any case, that too was acceptable then, both in the light of what was known at that time about the Mozarabs and because he was making assertions based on his data and the period which he had studied. But from this point on Menéndez Pidal launched into assumptions concerning the period after the

---

[15]Cano Aguilar (1998: 131–34).

eleventh century. This is where he prejudged what happened on the basis of his Castilian nationalist vision:

> Todo esto cambia con la hegemonía castellana que progresa desde el último tercio del siglo XI. El gran empuje que Castilla dio a la reconquista por Toledo y Andalucía y el gran desarrollo de la literatura y cultura castellanas trajeron consigo la propagación del dialecto castellano, antes poco difundido, el cual, al dilatarse hacia el Sur, desalojando de allí a los empobrecidos y moribundos dialectos mozárabes, rompió el lazo de unión que antes existía entre los dos extremos oriental y occidental e hizo cesar la primitiva continuidad geográfica de ciertos rasgos comunes del Oriente y el Occidente que hoy aparecen extrañamente aislados entre sí.
>
> La constitución de la lengua literaria española depende esencialmente de este fenómeno [...]: la nota diferencial castellana obra como una cuña que, clavada en el Norte, rompe la antigua unidad de ciertos caracteres comunes románicos antes extendidos por la Península y penetra hasta Andalucía, escindiendo alguna uniformidad dialectal, descuajando los primitivos caracteres lingüísticos del Duero a Gibraltar, esto es, borrando los dialectos mozárabes y en gran parte también los leoneses y aragoneses, y ensanchando cada vez más su acción de Norte a Sur para implantar la modalidad especial lingüística nacida en el norte cántabro. *La gran expansión de la lengua castellana no se realiza sino después del siglo XI, es decir, después de la fecha que nos hemos impuesto como término a este estudio.* (My italics; 1950³: 513–14)

There is increasing evidence that this expansion of Castilian was not as straightforward a process as Menéndez Pidal thought; his vision was far too dependent on his desire to allot to Castile the hegemonic and leading role. He also based his hypothesis exclusively on phonetic data. It is probably necessary to understand many of the changes which transformed Old Castilian into Spanish in a Peninsular context, as the result of linguistic innovations of Western or Eastern origin which ended up by prevailing also in the Central areas, or as an outcome of linguistic 'levelling' of the different dialects.[16]

---

[16]The number of those who support the theory of dialect levelling as a result of the repopulation process, rather than simple Castilianization, is rising; see Ridruejo (1995), Penny (2004), Tuten (2003), Enguita Utrilla (2008). Menéndez Pidal was also in favour of this idea: 'Cuando se produce la conquista de Andalucía y Murcia, se

Despite not taking into account any aspects of historical dialectology other than the phonetic, and any textual evidence other than the literary, Menéndez Pidal managed to establish his oversimplified view of the history of the Spanish language from the thirteenth century on. This vision has meant that subsequently only a very few scholars have made the effort to formulate a dialectal account of the history of the Spanish language. The paradoxical consequence is that the scholar who founded historical Spanish dialectology was also the one who demolished the chance that it would flourish with reference to the period following the eleventh century.

This outcome was undoubtedly determined by the overall acceptance of two of Menéndez Pidal's criteria for evaluating the evidence which are, at the very least, debatable. As he saw it, literary language was the benchmark for the development of the common language;[17] and, secondly, only phonetic data could be used to assess each variety's linguistic lineage. The following example is only one among many which could be chosen to illustrate his method of reasoning:

> Todo este dialectalismo [leonés o aragonés] se ve cada vez más minado en todas partes por la intrusión de formas extrañas, sobre todo por el avance de los castellanismos: primero, el

---

habían unido para siempre Castilla y León, así que la repoblación se hace con gentes mezcladas de los dos reinos, sin separación territorial entre gallegos, leoneses o castellanos, mezcla favorable a los influjos dialectales que integran la lengua común' (2005: 491). Nevertheless, he always claimed that the basis for the prevailing variety was Castilian, as can be demonstrated by his comments on dialect mixing in Toledo after its reconquest: 'Junto a los mozárabes (y los musulmanes y judíos, que en el reino toledano permanecieron o concurrieron a él) se establecieron, desde la conquista, como pobladores diferenciados los "castellanos" (nombre bajo el cual se incluían ya indistintamente tanto los procedentes del reino de León como a los procedentes del reino de Castilla y a los de las Extremaduras) y los "francos". Con el paso del tiempo, la legislación mozárabe del *Fuero Juzgo*, rechazada al principio por los pobladores castellanos, se fue generalizando en el curso de los siglos XII y XIII para todos. En cuanto al lenguaje ocurrió lo contrario, la lengua vulgar fue unificándose sobre base castellana' (2005: 453).

[17]Del Valle (1999, 2004) is right to analyse Menéndez Pidal as ascribing greater value to the language of written culture than to speech; that is, his tendency to identify the language with the standard, and to subordinate to it any other possible variety. But he fails to realize that this prejudice of Menéndez Pidal's had its origin in the basic role which he attributed to it as the medium for literature. As we have seen in note 9 above, Menéndez Pidal thought that 'La lengua no sigue al imperio, como decía Nebrija; la lengua sigue a la cultura'.

> diptongo *ué* se impone a las vacilaciones *o, uo, ua*; luego la *ch*
> se propaga rápidamente, excluyendo a la *t* etimológica; algo
> más tarde, la *j* va arrinconando a la *ll* o *y* antigua. Todas estas
> grandes innovaciones castellanas, que van descomponiendo
> y arruinando los dialectos literarios, señalan el fin de la edad
> primitiva del idioma. Pero Castilla, en suma, va haciendo
> respecto al idioma lo que había hecho respecto a la política
> durante el siglo anterior, combatir el estado de cosas propio
> de la Alta Edad Media para instaurar un orden nuevo. El
> castellano se ha impuesto ya a los dialectos circunvecinos,
> y pronto acabará con los sincretismos primitivos así como
> con el polidialectalismo literario. *Pero claro es que Castilla,*
> *fuera de la literatura, tenía mucho menos fuerza para acabar con el*
> *dialectalismo.* Los dialectos continuaron no sólo dominando en
> la lengua familiar de varias regiones, sino en la lengua escrita
> no literaria. (My italics; 2005: 482–83)

The postulated expansion of Castilian is based exclusively on phonetic data. Its imposition over the dialects of neighbouring areas
is taken as proved, despite the fact that it is not documented in
literature before the mid-thirteenth century nor in notarial documents until much later. And since Menéndez Pidal regarded it as
established that Castilian was the most suitable mode for written
representation from the mid-thirteenth century onward, he preferred
to ignore the evidence of non-literary texts, which were less likely
to conform to his theory of the leading role of Castilian, and to
concentrate on the evolution of the literary language alone, considering this to be the fundamental basis for the standardization of the
common language. This might be the reason why his *Documentos*
lingüísticos de España, which distinguish as many as fifteen different
Castilian areas (La Montaña, Campó, Castilla del Norte, Rioja, Álava,
Burgos, Osma, Valladolid and Cerrato, Segovia and Ávila, Sigüenza,
Toledo, Cuenca, Plasencia, Andalusia and Murcia) hardly include
documents from the fourteenth and fifteenth centuries; there are 271
from the thirteenth century, compared with 42 from the fourteenth
and 16 from the fifteenth. This reluctance to show the potential dialectal variety of Castilian documents from these periods is explained
by Menéndez Pidal with the following value judgement:

> porque de ese tiempo ya los textos literarios castellanos se
> conservan en gran número y la lengua restringida y cada vez

> más amanerada de los notarios pierde casi todo su interés
> frente a la más rica de los escritores de varia índole que
> entonces abundan. (1966²: V–VI)

The decline of Leonese in the modern era is also explained, according
to Menéndez Pidal, by literature being the benchmark:

> En el antiguo reino de León, Asturias ofrece una producción
> literaria mínima, casi nula, y Galicia muy poca. Y aunque
> exceden con mucho a esas dos, las otras regiones del reino,
> considerando éste en conjunto durante la edad del español
> clásico, muestran una fecundidad bastante menor (244 au-
> tores) que la de Castilla la Vieja (450 autores) o Castilla la
> Nueva (519 autores), con ser cada una de estas territorio
> menor que el del reino leonés. Esto por sí solo explica la
> supremacía incontrastable del patrón lingüístico castellano.
> (2005: 701)

For the same reason, Menéndez Pidal placed no importance on
the inconvenient Aragonese medieval literature overseen by Juan
Fernández de Heredia, in case the suspicion might arise that it
could have overshadowed Castilian, explaining that it was copying
foreign models rather than representing genuine Aragonese literary
tendencies:

> La más importante acción cultural del reino de Aragón no pro-
> cede de su propia entraña (casi estéril en la época medieval),
> sino de importación externa. (2005: 595)

As if a significant part of medieval Castilian literature, including the
epic, had not also been subject to external influence!

V. Spanish is the result of the evolution of the three central romance dialects on the Iberian Peninsula

This view of Castilian's leading role in the linguistic evolution of
the Peninsula has come to be firmly held not only by Menéndez
Pidal's supporters but also by his critics. As a consequence of
the unconditional acceptance of his ideas by his supporters, the
possibility that Astur-Leonese or Navarro-Aragonese (not to mention Galician-Portuguese or Catalan) might have contributed to the
formation of the Spanish language has never been considered, in
such a way that evidence from these has frequently been ignored
by those researching the history of the Spanish language, which in

turn has become exclusively the history of the Castilian language. The acceptance of Menéndez Pidal's views by his critics, on the other hand, does not only consist of the identification of Spanish with Castilian, but also of the belief that Spanish (Castilian) was a foreign language outside the borders of Castile; i.e. that it invaded linguistically distinct territories and subjugated them to a process of Castilianization. Both his supporters and critics forget that in addition to his persistently biased view that the Castilian was the core and essence of everything Hispanic, Menéndez Pidal always maintained the idea that Spanish (or 'the common Spanish language', *la lengua común española*, as he sometimes called it) evolved from a Castilian base which would have absorbed, or merged with, Leonese and Aragonese. If we read his *Historia de la lengua*, it becomes clear that he was keen to explain the stages of this process.[18] In contrast, the process by which Spanish was created was only touched on tangentially by Rafael Lapesa in his own *Historia de la lengua*, because by that time his mentor's Castilian nationalist views had become so deeply ingrained that, as can be deduced from the structure of the book, the history of the Spanish language is considered to refer to the history of Castilian, from the thirteenth century on, without considering the problem of the way in which the old dialects had come to disappear, nor their territories' subsequent Castilianization, nor the possibility that in this process those dialects might have influenced the evolution of 'the common Spanish language'.[19]

---

[18]Apart from the sections mentioned above in note 8, other examples that show his interest in the contribution of Leonese and Aragonese to the formation of the common Spanish language include: part IV, chapter VI 'Estado de la lengua común', 1. 'Relativa estabilidad', 2. 'La lengua común. Toledo y Sevilla', 4. 'Los dialectos laterales y el dialecto central'; chapter VII 'Período de transición (1370–1400)', 1. 'Influjo galaico-leonés. Romances y arte mayor', 2. 'Ensayos humanísticos en aragonés: Fernández de Heredia'; part V, chapter II 'Los dialectos viejos completan su nacionalización', 1. 'Ojeada general', 2. 'La unidad política y el reino de Aragón', 3. 'El reino de León', 4. 'Castilla la Nueva. Toledo y la corte como normas uniformadoras'. We should add to these, as examples of the analysis of phenomena liable to dialectal variation, the sections dedicated to Andalusian individuality and to the phonetics of Old Castilian.

[19]Comparing the two books entitled *Historia de la lengua*, by Menéndez Pidal and Lapesa, brings to light important similarities and differences (cf. Arenas Olleta 2007 as regards their methods of periodization). In addition to the attention given to Leonese and Aragonese, another significant difference lies in the greater

Already at the beginning of the twentieth century Menéndez Pidal was aware that he would have to take some account of the Leonese and the Aragonese dialects in order to explain 'Spanish'. In the above-mentioned letter to Unamuno, written in 1903, it can be seen that he thought he could tackle the history of the Spanish language only after having studied Leonese and Aragonese. In his *Manual de gramática histórica* he states:

> El castellano, por servir de instrumento a una literatura más importante que la de otras regiones de España, y sobre todo por haber absorbido en sí otros dos romances principales hablados en la Península (el leonés y el navarro-aragonés) recibe más propiamente el nombre de lengua española. (1940[6]: 2)

As is generally known, this was how he presented his case successfully to the Real Academia Española, and unsuccessfully to those who were drawing up the Constitution of the Second Republic. The preeminence of Castilian is said once again to have been ensured by its being the main language for the expression of Spanish literature; but what I want to emphasize here is that he considered it inappropriate to speak about a 'Castilian' language since he acknowledged that the result, the 'common Spanish language', also contained Leonese and Navarro-Aragonese elements. This became clearer when he discussed loanwords taken from other Romance languages into Castilian:

> Las otras hablas de España más afines al castellano y que se fundieron con él para formar la lengua literaria, dieron también a ésta muchísimas palabras; pero son difíciles de reconocer, pues como estos dialectos afines tienen la mayoría de sus leyes fonéticas comunes con el castellano, tales palabras no llevan sello de evolución especial. (1940: 27)

In this passage we can highlight the importance, mentioned previously, that was conferred on phonetics by Menéndez Pidal. Although he genuinely envisaged the evolution of Spanish as a complex

---

attention devoted to history in general by Menéndez Pidal from the thirteenth century onwards, consistent with the overall plan of his *Historia*, whereas from the fourteenth century Lapesa hardly mentions the general historical framework, in order to concentrate instead on literary and cultural history (see Cano Aguilar 2009). Wright, in this volume, also points out the greater attention paid to modern linguistic history in Menéndez Pidal's *Historia* as compared with Lapesa's *Historia*.

process, he admits his inability to identify exactly how each linguistic area contributed to this process when basing almost all of his conclusions on phonetic arguments.

The title itself of *Orígenes del español* is illuminating as regards Menéndez Pidal's conception of the common Spanish language; they are not the origins of Castilian but of Spanish. The *Glosas emilianenses* were, according to Menéndez Pidal, written in Spanish Romance ('romance español') despite their clear Navarro-Aragonese features:

> Esta zona es la patria de las Glosas Emilianenses en que un monje mezcla el naciente idioma español con unas frases en vasco [...]. Las Glosas [...] son el primer texto en que el romance español quiere ser escrito con total independencia del latín. (1950³: 225 & 470)

In line with this perspective, the book analyses data from the linguistic areas of the central Iberian Peninsula from León to Aragón, which he considered to be the basis of Spanish, whereas Galician-Portuguese and Catalan are almost completely overlooked.

To show that to some extent he believed in the linguistic assimilation (levelling) of the Peninsula's central dialects, it can be pointed out that he considered, for instance, that the decision not to represent apocope in the common literary language, which he dedicated many sections of his *Historia de la lengua* to, was the result of Leonese influence (again, this is a phonetic phenomenon). In his analysis of the dialectalisms present in the works of Alfonso X he states:

> En la misma *General Estoria* (manuscrito vaticano) aparece otro leonesismo que más especialmente nos interesa: *piedade, salude*, indicio de que el leonés echa el peso de su tradicional autoridad en contra de la apócope de la vocal final que el castellano extremaba; el leonés, veremos que obtendrá un triunfo en ese terreno. En sintaxis se observa más abundantemente el influjo leonés, generalizando la interpolación de una palabra, a veces más de una, entre el pronombre átono y el verbo [...]. Es un uso irradiado desde el Occidente de la Península, pues estas interpolaciones tienen su máximo uso en el gallego portugués, donde aún hoy subsisten; luego abundan en el leonés antiguo, y son desconocidas, o casi, en el aragonés. Su boga en Castilla se ha de deber a influjo galaico-leonés. (2005: 532)

When discussing the apocope of the pronouns *me* and *te* in the *Libro de buen amor*, he indicates that in every instance:

> ocurren en la parte de las serranillas, sin duda representando la lengua rústica de Guadarrama, a la cual no había llegado la influencia leonesa adversa a la apócope. (2005: 577)

During the transition from the fourteenth to the fifteenth centuries, Menéndez Pidal again affirms the contribution made by Leonese to Spanish language and literature by relating the rejection of apocope to the success of two new metrical forms, the romance and the *octavas* of *Arte Mayor*, which replaced the previous traditional poetic forms:

> El leonés vencerá por completo en cuanto a la apócope, como en otros puntos, pero ya no hay clara conciencia de que represente un dialecto aparte. (2005: 584)

> Con estas dos invenciones métricas [romance y arte mayor], la lengua española había encontrado su propio ritmo en frases o hemistiquios de 6 y 8 sílabas […]. Este cambio de versificación sin duda se relaciona con el olvido de la apócope, o sea, con la conservación de la *–e* final latina que, por influjo principal de León, dio al idioma su nuevo y definitivo ritmo; no es por esto de extrañar el influjo del reino leonés en la constitución de los dos metros de Romance y de Arte Mayor. (2005: 594)

He grants León the leading role in the disappearance of non-verbal apocope:

> Durante cuatro siglos el dialecto central castellano vacila entre el leonés y el aragonés respecto a la conservación o pérdida de la *–e* final, cediendo por fin a la tendencia leonesa, como era de esperar, dada la antigua unidad política de los reinos de Castilla y de León. (2005: 645)

This absence, which was 'as would be expected' ('como era de esperar') is, of course, not at all what we would expect in the light of Menéndez Pidal's continual insistence that on the whole it was Castilian forms which prevailed. Compared with this recognition of the contribution made by Leonese, based on documentary evidence, there does not seem to be any case in which Aragonese is presented to us as playing the winning role in the formation of Spanish, except for the odd lexical item such as *entremés*, *faxa* or *arrollar* (2005: 646 & 698). This lack of Aragonese influence seems to be linked to the fact that Menéndez Pidal's working methodology was mainly based on phonetic differences, since he was unable to find traces of authentic Aragonese phonetic phenomena in the common literary language (unlike the loss of *apócope extrema*, which was a Western characteristic).

Nevertheless, we cannot rule out that the possibility that there was an underlying tendency in his account not to focus on, or to downplay, possible Aragonese contributions as compared to those of Leonese. This is noticeable, for instance, in his reconstruction of the development and diffusion of the phonological system of Modern Spanish. In his *Historia de la lengua* he insistently attributes the responsibility for the new pronunciations to the phonetics of Old Castilian, despite the fact with the phrase 'Old Castilian' he is actually referring to the pronunciation of Northern areas which include territories on the banks of the Ebro and the Duero settled by people coming from several different areas.

It is worth pointing out that, as Menéndez Pidal conceived it, Old Castile was limited to Cantabria and its neighbouring regions in the Middle Ages; and so, consistently with this reconstruction, he argued that the *Auto de los reyes magos* and the *Poema de Mio Cid* were not Castilian (2005: 468–72). However, after that period its territory expanded considerably; he considered as part of 'Old Castile' places which were part of the Kingdom of León until well into the Middle Ages, such as Valladolid and Palencia, and even areas located in Eastern León and in the Tierra de Campos. In this way Menéndez Pidal could consider to be an accurate representation of 'Old Castilian' pronunciation the evidence provided by Antonio de Torquemada, who is said to 'hacerlo conforme al uso y estilo de la casa de Benavente', despite being aware that:

> Torquemada [...] parece describirnos la pronunciación más autorizada de su tierra, esto es, desde el Esla (Benavente) hasta el Pisuerga (Torquemada) en cuyo centro está tierra de Campos (Mayorga) (2005: 880);

that is, in territories that belonged to the Kingdom of León until the mid-twelfth century.[20] Regardless of where Torquemada, the author of the *Manual de escribientes*, actually was, time after time

---

[20]The areas between the rivers Cea and Pisuerga were only incorporated into Castile after Sancho III el Mayor took them away from León in 1034 (Fernando I inheriting

Menéndez Pidal insisted that the modern pronunciation originated in Old Castile (2005: 875–87 & 995–1017); and he maintained that because of its influence:

> Desde luego los dialectos afines al español literario, el astur-leonés y el navarro-aragonés, ensordecieron contemporánea-mente sus fricativas *j*, *z*, *s*. (2005: 1016)

Even though he acknowledged in a note that 'casos esporádicos de ensordecimiento ocurrían desde época antiquísima en aragonés' (2005: 1016, n. 47), no attempt was made to connect this with the evolution of Castilian; and there is no discussion of the linguistic features found in works by authors from Navarre or Aragón who were writing at the same time as the Castilians whose language is commented on extensively and in detail.

---

them as part of Castile); or possibly even as late as 1157, when Alfonso VII's lands were divided, in the opinion of Martínez Sopena (1985: 13–14). Either way, the incorporation into Castile took place long after the initial medieval colonization of that region in the ninth and tenth centuries, which makes it unlikely that the political frontier could have had any linguistic consequences. This makes it surprising that those areas have been taken to belong linguistically to Castile, and are never included as part of the Leonese linguistic area, despite the fact that many features that are thought to be Leonese in origin are also commonly found in Palencia, Valladolid and even Burgos (see, for example, the studies in Morala 2008). This is the case, for example, with the analogical strong perfects (Pato 2004b, 2009) or of *leísmo* for masculine count nouns, which group together the Eastern Leonese area with Castile within an isogloss which coincides with that of the conservation of initial F-and the palatalization of L-, separating Central from Eastern Leonese (Fernández-Ordóñez 2001: 449–54). In many ways Castilian is just the dialect which developed in the Eastern part of the Kingdom of León. Being varieties spoken in the same kingdom, as part of the same dialect continuum, it is impossible to establish clear frontiers between Galician and Astur-Leonese, or between Astur-Leonese and Castilian, at least for those areas in which Latin had developed in situ from ancient times, or which were repopulated before the twelfth century, as both Neira (1989), discussing a number of linguistic features, and Penny (2004b), rightly point out. But as in studies on the history of Castilian, Menéndez Pidal's prestige can still be seen today in the fact that those who study Asturian and Leonese still follow the boundaries that he proposed for the dialects in 1906, in *El dialecto leonés*, basing those on the political borders of the Kingdom of León at the start of the thirteenth century; the consequence is that they do not consider the data from the territories in Eastern León that are situated north of the Duero (Cantabria, Burgos, Palencia and Valladolid), and thus do not take into account the fact that many features found there are the same.

VI. Conclusion

As early as 1916, in his review of Griera's study of the Catalan-Aragonese border, Menéndez Pidal developed a typology of the different kinds of dialect border, which is still in essence in effect today; as far as I can see, it was deployed then for the first time ever with reference to the study of the Peninsular Romance languages. In that review, Menéndez Pidal made a distinction between two different kinds of isoglosses; those that do not coincide and criss-cross each other, which characterize a transitional zone, and those that do coincide, forming a bundle, and which thus delimit clearly two different linguistic areas:

> A veces observamos varios límites confundidos en un haz o conjunto de líneas que marchan juntas en toda o gran parte de su extensión: límites coincidentes, que obedecen a la irra-diación de grandes masas de fenómenos lingüísticos; es decir, una porción de fenómenos fonéticos, morfológicos o sintácti-cos alcanzan un mismo límite llevados por el mismo impulso propagador. La coincidencia de los límites es por lo común el resultado del choque de dos lenguas o dialectos que se sienten entre sí como diversos; hay conciencia de la distinción entre las lenguas colindantes y ambas se excluyen mutuamente en gran parte de sus fenómenos característicos [...]. Pero más, por lo común, observamos que los límites siguen direcciones muy varias, entrecruzándose de muy diverso modo; estos límites obedecen a irradiaciones parciales dentro de un medio lingüístico relativamente homogéneo, capaz de ser afectado por esta especie de movimientos ondulatorios que se propa-gan, cada uno según su impulso independiente, a diversas distancias y en diversas direcciones [...]. En España esta diferencia tiene una aplicación muy importante cuando se estudian las fronteras de los dialectos románicos del norte. Los límites lingüísticos entre el leonés y el gallego desde el Cantábrico hasta hacia el Duero, o los del aragonés y el catalán desde los Pirineos hasta hacia Benabarre, son principalmente sueltos o entrecruzados, mientras que más al sur son límites por lo general coincidentes. (1916: 77–78)

The most interesting aspect of this double distinction is that it has consequences concerning whether we think that the linguistic variety in question is genuinely native or has come from elsewhere, taking into account what we know about Peninsular history:

> al norte de la región los límites fonéticos van por lo general
> sueltos y [...] al sur todos ellos se juntan en un haz a partir de
> cierto punto. Al norte tenemos el resultado de la evolución
> ininterrumpida de dialectos románicos primitivos, y al sur
> el resultado de una invasión en masa debida principalmente,
> como es de presumir, a la reconquista, invasión de una lengua
> completa que se propaga desplazando a otra preexistente.
> (1916: 79)

This historical interpretation of the dialectal framework of the Peninsula has been generally accepted by all those who study the history
of the different Ibero-Romance languages, distinguishing the dialect
continuum in the North from areas with clearer dialect borders
further south (e.g. Penny 2004a). Even so, the same Menéndez Pidal
who postulated this in order to explain the pattern of the geographical distribution of the isoglosses between Galician-Portuguese, Spanish and Catalan, was unable to put it into practice when he was
studying the central dialects which he considered to form the basis of
Spanish: that is, Astur-Leonese, Castilian and Navarro-Aragonese.
This inability may well be due to the fact that his reasoning was
based, as we have seen many times already, on phonetic features.
But it is probably also to be explained by his assumption of the
'Castilianization' of the whole central and southern region, and the
disappearance of the transitional zones, which were replaced by a
homogeneous 'Castilian'. Since he had not identified those linguistic
features of Astur-Leonese and Aragonese which had coincided orig-
inally with those of Castilian, the linguistic source of the language
used in the central part of the Peninsula could be ascribed without
any problem to Castilian alone.[21]

   Menéndez Pidal's Castilian nationalism undoubtedly reflects the
ideological prejudices of the age, as well as the role he ascribed to
Castile in the literary expression of Spanish national identity. We
should therefore discount it, as being a prejudice, as prejudging the
issues, since it is, in any event, based on an exclusively phonetic
analysis of the linguistic features. But more than that, it is not clear,
even as regards pronunciation, that his famous *cuña castellana* ever

---

[21]For example, Menéndez Pidal regarded as exclusively Castilian the language
spoken to the north of the Duero in Palencia or Valladolid, even though it is only
after 1157 that we can be sure that those areas belonged administratively to Castile:
see note 20 above.

existed, since that could only ever be deduced on the basis of the incomplete knowledge of dialect phonetics that there was between 1920 and 1950. The data had not then been published then, indeed they have never been published, which would have enabled linguists to work out a complete dialect map of the Peninsula; that is, the data that were used for the *Atlas lingüístico de la Península Ibérica* (*ALPI*), which should be regarded as a unique treasure, since they are the only data which organise the whole of the peninsula in one common grid, however imperfectly.[22] If those data had been known at the time, they would have shown a far more complex reality than that of the Castilian 'wedge'.

That complexity has already been pointed out by Navarro Tomás, in his phonetic dialect geography studies published in 1975, after the first volume of the *ALPI* came out; and by Diego Catalán in his masterly article (also 1975) 'De Nájera a Salobreña. Notas históricas y lingüísticas sobre un reino en estado latente', where he analysed the only lexical map currently available in the *ALPI*: *aguijón*. Navarro Tomás's studies make it possible to see that many Western Castilian phonetic features coincide with those of Leonese regions (for instance, the reduced pronunciation of final -*s* and -*θ*, and the open articulation of stressed *o*), while the Basque Country, Navarre, Aragón and La Rioja coincide with Eastern Castile.[23] Thus there is

---

[22]Only one volume of the *ALPI* was published, in 1962. Its source materials went missing for more than four decades until they were eventually found by David Heap in 2002. The data are now available in the form of images on the Internet: Heap (2003).

[23]These are Navarro Tomás's conclusions to his analysis of the o in *boca*: 'Las zonas del catalán, aragonés y del castellano oriental excluyen visiblemente la variedad de tendencia abierta. Las del castellano occidental y del leonés rechazan la tendencia cerrada' (1975: 91). There is a similar division between two types of Castilian in the realization of final -*s*: 'La diferenciación entre las variedades plena y reducida de la final -*s* señala en Castilla dos zonas distintas. La -*s* plena en el mapa de árboles corresponde con raras excepciones a las provincias orientales de Logroño, Soria, Guadalajara, Cuenca y Albacete [articulación en que coinciden con Aragón y los territorios catalano-hablantes]; la reducida se da en las provincias centrales y occidentales de Santander, Burgos, Palencia, Valladolid, Segovia, Ávila, Madrid, Toledo y Ciudad Real' (1975: 189). The distribution of final -*z* is also very similar: 'La amplia extensión de la -*z* interdental comprende las provincias castellanas, leonesas y aragonesas. Se distinguen en la articulación de la final -*z*, como en la de la -*s*, una modalidad plena y otra reducida y débil. La zona más uniforme de -*z* plena incluye Navarra, La Rioja, Aragón, La Alcarria y Cuenca. Soria practica la modalidad

no such thing as a uniform Castilian in many respects, including phonetic ones. In this way it turns out that many of the phonetic developments which Menéndez Pidal considered to be exclusively Old Castilian could well have also at the same time been Navarrese, or Aragonese, or Leonese, and not because of a simple process of Castilianization; in the same way that, as early as the 1960s, scholars including Dámaso Alonso (1962) took it upon themselves to make clear that the medieval confusion of *b* and *v*, or the devoicing of sibilants, were complex processes in which Castilianization was not the main cause.[24]

Diego Catalán's article does not only demonstrate the existence of linguistic areas that fail to correspond with the leading role attributed to Castile by Menéndez Pidal; it also makes clear that when working out the dialect map of the Iberian Peninsula we should take into account not only phonetic but also lexical features. For my part, I would add that there is also a need to consider grammatical features. There are Castilian grammatical features, such as *leísmo*, which are only found in Eastern León, Western Castile and the Basque Country. The many phenomena related to the *neutro de materia*, which has been a feature of Castilian alone since the Middle Ages (Fernández-Ordóñez 1994, 2001, 2006–07), have not been welcomed into the standard language, nor in the Spanish spoken in most of the Peninsula. Neither do we find south of the Duero, in Castile, or south of the Ebro, in Navarra and La Rioja, a feature which has its focal area in the Eastern Castilian of Burgos, Vizcaya and La Rioja: the replacement of verb forms in *-ra* and *-se* by the conditional form *-ría*, despite its being well documented in that region during the Middle Ages (Pato 2004). Castilian features have not always prevailed in the development of the common language of the old medieval kingdoms of León, Aragón, Navarre, Castile, Toledo, Seville, Murcia

reducida, pero Logroño, Guadalajara y Cuenca, con variedad plena, contrastan con la atenuada predominante en Santander, Burgos, Palencia, Valladolid, Segovia, Ávila y Madrid. Se advierte también en este caso la mencionada diferencia entre el lado oriental de Castilla y el occidental, aunque con menos regularidad que en el de la *-s*. En Asturias, León, Zamora, Lugo y Orense, la *-z* interdental plena es más frecuente que la reducida, al contrario que Salamanca, adscrita a la variedad reducida de la Castilla occidental' (1975: 191–92).

[24]This is a view also held by many others: see Pascual (1996–97: 89–92) or Cano Aguilar (1998: 135–38; 2005).

and Jaén (as Alfonso X referred to them). Compound tenses, for example, originated in the East of the Peninsula, in Catalonia and Aragón (Rodríguez Molina 2004, 2008), and were used only later in the centre, firstly in the East of Castile. Thus even now in Galician and Asturian these forms are still unknown, while in the North of Castile and areas formerly in the Kingdom of León, as well as in Extremadura, Western Andalusia and Spanish America, the use of compound tenses is more limited today than in other areas or in standard peninsular Spanish. In turn, the replacement of *amase* with *amara* must have had its point of origin in the West of the peninsula, as evidenced by Asturian, the speech varieties of the former Kingdom of León and Western Andalusia, and Atlantic Spanish, in all of which *amase* has been completely replaced with *amara* as a subjunctive form, whereas in the mountains of Aragón *amase* is preferred (cf. Alvar 1979–83). The same argument can be made as regards many other features. Many of the linguistic changes which transformed medieval varieties into modern ones, if contemplated from a straightforward Peninsular-wide perspective that takes into account the coexisting evidence of all Ibero-Romance languages, could be explained by hypotheses concerning the focal areas of the expansion of modern features which have barely been considered up to the present day. Without denying the occasional existence of a Castilian wedge,[25] we should acknowledge that we can also see a Castilian-Leonese wedge,[26] a Castilian-Navarro-Aragonese wedge,[27] and sometimes one that groups together the whole central Leonese-Castilian-Aragonese area.[28] There are also areas into which

---

[25]As well as the lexical map for *mustela* which was included in the second edition of the *Orígenes* (cf. Pato 2007), the geographical distribution of the *-illo* diminutive also fits the pattern of the Castilian wedge, as the *ALPI* questionnaires allow us to see.

[26]That grouping is probably operative as regards the replacement of *amase* by *amara*, or the use of the periphrastic future (*ir* + infinitive) rather than the synthetic.

[27]The linguistic studies of thirteenth-century Teruel are very significant in this respect; in those documents and fueros both Castilian and Aragonese phonetic developments are attested (Enguita Utrilla 2008). Since Navarrese and Aragonese participated in the repopulation of Teruel in equal numbers, this seems to indicate that by that time the Navarrese already used a type of language which was predominantly 'Castilian', despite being politically independent of Castile at that time.

[28]This possibility was suggested by Pascual (1996–97) or Cano Aguilar: 'En los muchos casos de diferencias dialectales (históricas y modernas) basadas en la

the Castilian wedge has not expanded, stopping sharply at the Duero or the Tagus, and remains anchored in an area of still uncertain linguistic affiliation.[29] The linguistic levelling between those who came from several different dialect areas to repopulate that no man's land was probably such a decisive factor in the formation of the ensuing linguistic characteristics of the area that the result cannot simply be ascribed to Castilian influence, or indeed the influence of anywhere in particular.

The conclusion should be that linguistic developments can only be correctly interpreted in a comparative context. If the Romance languages on the Iberian Peninsula have frequently been overlooked during research into Spanish, that is clearly a result of the Spanish School of Philology being so heavily imbued with the Castilian nationalism of Menéndez Pidal that it may well have been taken further than he intended. It is the duty of the philologists and linguists of the twenty-first century to remedy this.

Works Cited

ALONSO, Dámaso, 1962. *Temas y problemas de la fragmentación fonética peninsular* (Madrid: CSIC).

ALVAR, Manuel, 1979–83. *Atlas lingüístico y etnográfico de Aragón, Navarra y La Rioja*, con la colaboración de Antonio Llorente, Tomás Buesa y Elena Alvar, 12 vols (Zaragoza: Institución Fernando el Católico / CSIC).

---

morfología, en especial la verbal, tampoco se trata de que el castellano desplazara desde el principio unas formas que, ante su empuje, quedaran arrinconadas en los márgenes: por el contrario, el castellano compartió muchas de esas formas en la época antigua, e incluso después. [...] en el plano sintáctico [...] este dialecto vuelve a estar acompañado por los vecinos: del leonés al aragonés, con el castellano como elemento central, la imagen de homogeneidad interna y de mutua comunidad sintáctica es completa. Los dialectos centrales forman en este sentido un bloque compacto, en el que comparten fenómenos como el empleo de a ante Objeto Directo en condiciones idénticas, el uso de los tiempos y modos verbales, los mecanismos y modos específicos de rección y complementación oracional e interoracional...' (1998: 138–39). Although I do not agree with Cano Aguilar that there is complete syntactic uniformity among the central dialects, it is true that they share many features different from those of Galician-Portuguese and/or Catalan.

[29]The replacement of the subjunctive by the conditional has not crossed south of the Duero; and the pronominal distinction between count and mass has not gone much further south than the Tagus (as I pointed out above).

ARENAS OLLETA, Julio, 2007. 'Lapesa y Pidal, dos historias de la lengua', in *Mit Clio im Gespräch. Romanische Sprachgeschichten und Sprachgeschichtschreibung*, ed. Jochen Hafner and Wulf Oesterreicher (Tübingen: Gunter Narr), pp. 233–54.

Atlas lingüístico de la Península Ibérica (*ALPI*): NAVARRO TOMÁS, Tomás, dir., 1962. *Atlas lingüístico de la Península Ibérica*, vol. 1, *Fonética*, con la colaboración de Francesc de Borja MOLL, Aurelio M. ESPINOSA [junior], Luís F. LINDLEY CINTRA, Armando NOBRE DE GUSMÃO, Aníbal OTERO, Lorenzo RODRÍGUEZ CASTELLANO y Manuel SANCHIS GUARNER (Madrid: CSIC).

ARMISTEAD, Samuel G., 2001. 'Menéndez Pidal, the epic and the generation of "98"', *C*, 29: 33–57.

CANO AGUILAR, Rafael, 1998. 'Los orígenes del español: nuevos planteamientos', in *Estudios de lingüística y filología españolas. Homenaje a Germán Colón*, ed. I. Andrés-Suárez and Luis López Molina (Madrid: Gredos), pp. 127–40.

——, 2005. 'Cambios en la fonología del español durante los siglos XVI y XVII', in *Historia de la lengua española*, ed. R. Cano (Madrid: Ariel), pp. 825–57.

——, 2009. 'Lapesa y la concepción de la historia de la lengua para el español', in *La obra de Lapesa desde la filología actual*, ed. J.J. Bustos and R. Cano, (Madrid: Sociedad Estatal de Conmemoraciones Culturales), pp. 483–508.

CASTRO, Américo & Federico de ONÍS, 1916. *Fueros leoneses de Zamora, Salamanca, Ledesma y Alba de Tormes* (Madrid: Centro de Estudios Históricos).

CATALÁN, Diego, 1975. 'De Nájera a Salobreña. Notas lingüísticas e históricas sobre un reino en estado latente', in *Studia Hispanica in Honorem R. Lapesa*, III (Madrid: Seminario Menéndez Pidal / Gredos), pp. 97–121. Reprinted in *El español. Orígenes de su diversidad*, 1989 (Madrid: Paraninfo), pp. 296–327.

——, 2005. 'Una catedral para una lengua', in R. MENÉNDEZ PIDAL(2005), vol. II, pp. 77–354.

CATALÁN, Diego & Álvaro GALMÉS DE FUENTES, 1954, 1989[2]. 'La diptongación en leonés', *Archivum*, 4: 87–147. Reprinted in *Las lenguas circunvecinas del castellano*, 1989 (Madrid: Paraninfo), pp. 167–206.

CID, Jesús Antonio, 1991. 'Una encuesta en Guernica (1920–1921). Menéndez Pidal, el romancero y los nacionalismos ibéricos', in *Memoriae L. Mitxelena Magistri Sacrum*, ed. J. A. Lakarra, I. Ruiz Arzalluz (San Sebastián: Diputación Foral de Guipúzcoa), pp. 527–52.

DEL VALLE, José, 1999. 'Lenguas imaginadas: Menéndez Pidal, la lingüística hispánica y la configuración del estándar', *BHS*, 76: 215–33.

——, 2004. 'Menéndez Pidal, la regeneración nacional y la utopía lingüística', in *La batalla del idioma: la intelectualidad hispánica ante la lengua*, ed.   José del Valle and Luis Gabriel-Stheeman, (Madrid / Frankfurt: Iberoamericana / Vervuert), pp. 109–36.

EGIDO FERNÁNDEZ, María Cristina, 2003. 'Algunos aspectos gramaticales en documentación astur-leonesa', in *Lengua romance en textos latinos de la Edad Media*, ed. Hermógenes Perdiguero Villareal (Burgos: Universidad de Burgos / Instituto Castellano y Leonés de la Lengua), pp. 49–69.

ENGUITA UTRILLA, José María, 2008.   'Sobre el aragonés medieval', in *Lenguas, reinos y dialectos en la Edad Media Ibérica*, ed. Javier Elvira, Inés Fernández-Ordóñez, Javier García & Ana Serradilla (Madrid / Frankfurt: Iberoamericana / Vervuert), pp. 83–106.

FERNÁNDEZ-ORDÓÑEZ, Inés, 1994. 'Isoglosas internas del castellano.   El sistema referencial del pronombre átono de tercera persona', *RFE*, 74: 71–125.

——, 2001. 'Hacia una dialectología histórica. Reflexiones sobre la historia del leísmo, el laísmo y el loísmo', *Boletín de la Real Academia Española*, 81: 389–464.

——, 2006. 'Contribuciones de Ramón Menéndez Pidal al estudio del catalán: del *I Congrés Internacional de la Llengua Catalana al Atlas Lingüístico de la Península Ibérica*', in *El Primer Congrés Internacional de la Llengua Catalana. Reflexos i projeccions*, ed. Maria Pilar Perea and Germà Colón Domènech (Barcelona / Castelló de la Plana: PPU), pp. 173–202.

——, 2006–07. 'Del Cantábrico a Toledo. El "neutro de materia" hispánico en un contexto románico y tipológico', *Revista de Historia de la Lengua Española*, 1: 67–118; 2: 29–81.

FORNEIRO, José Luis, 2000. *El romancero tradicional de Galicia: una poesía entre dos lenguas* (Oiartzun: Sendoa).

——, 2004. *Allá em riba un rey tinha una filha. Galego e castelhano no romanceiro da Galiza* (Ourense: Difusora).

——, 2005. 'Presença da língua castelhana na literatura popular galega', *Agália: Publicaçom internacional da Associaçom Galega da Lingua*, 81–82: 97–120.

——, 2010. 'Linguistic borders and oral transmission', in *A Comparative History of Literatures in the Iberian Peninsula*, ed. Fernando Cabo Aseguinolaza (Amsterdam: John Benjamins), in press.

GARATEA GRAU, Carlos, 2005. *El problema del cambio lingüístico en Ramón Menéndez Pidal. El individuo, las tradiciones y la historia* (Tübingen: Gunter Narr Verlag).

GARCÍA ISASTI, Prudencio, 2004. *La España metafísica. Lectura crítica del pensamiento de Ramón Menéndez Pidal (1891–1936)* (Bilbao: Universidad del País Vasco / Real Academia de la Lengua Vasca).

GERLI, E. Michael, 2001. 'Inventing the Spanish Middle Ages: Ramón Menéndez Pidal, Spanish cultural history, and ideology in philology', *C*, 30: 111–26.

Heap, David, 2002. 'Segunda noticia histórica del ALPI (a los cuarenta años de la publicación de su primer tomo)', *RFE*, 82: 5–19.

——, 2003. *Atlas lingüístico de la Península Ibérica. ALPI searchable database* (London, Ontario: University of Western Ontario) (http://www.alpi.ca).

Hess, Steven, 1996. '"Castilian hegemony": Linguistics and Politics in *Orígenes del español*', *C*, 24: 114–22.

Lapesa, Rafael, 1981⁹. *Historia de la Lengua española* (Madrid: Gredos).

Martínez Sopena, Pascual, 1985. *La Tierra de Campos occidental. Poblamiento, poder y comunidad del siglo X al XIII* (Valladolid: Diputación Provincial).

Matute Martínez, Cristina, 2004. *Los sistemas pronominales en español antiguo. Problemas y métodos para una reconstrucción histórica* (Madrid: Universidad Autónoma / Ed. de la Autora). (http://www.ffil.uam.es/coser/publicaciones/cristina/1_es.pdf).

Menéndez Pidal, Ramón, 1902. 'Poema de Yuçuf. Materiales para su estudio', *RABM*, 7: 91–129, 276–309, 347–62; reprinted in *Textos medievales españoles. Ediciones críticas y estudios* (Madrid: Espasa-Calpe), 1976, pp. 421–519.

——, 1904, 1940⁶. *Manual de gramática histórica española* (Madrid: Espasa-Calpe).

——, 1905. 'Razón de Amor con los Denuestos del agua y el vino', *Revue Hispanique*, 13: 602–18; reprinted in *Textos medievales españoles. Ediciones críticas y estudios* (Madrid: Espasa-Calpe), 1976, pp. 103–17.

——, 1906. 'El dialecto leonés', *Revista de Archivos, Bibliotecas y Museos*, 14: 128–72, 294–311; reprinted as *El dialecto leonés* (Oviedo: Instituto de Estudios Asturianos), with prologue, notes and appendices by Carmen Bobes, 1962.

——, 1908–11, 1976–80⁵. *Cantar de Mio Cid. Texto, gramática y vocabulario*, 3 vols (Madrid: Espasa-Calpe).

——, 1914. '*Elena y María (Disputa del clérigo y el caballero)*. Poesía leonesa inédita del siglo XIII', *RFE*, 1: 52–96; reprinted in *Textos medievales españoles. Ediciones críticas y estudios* (Madrid: Espasa-Calpe), 1976, pp. 119–59.

——, 1916. Review of A. Griera i Gaja, *La frontera catalano-aragonesa. Estudi Geogràfico-Lingüístic* (Barcelona: Institut d'Estudis Catalans, 1914), *Revista de Filología Española*, 3: 73–88.

——, 1917. 'Roncesvalles. Un nuevo cantar de gesta español del siglo XIII', *RFE*, 4: 105–204; reprinted in *Textos medievales españoles. Ediciones críticas y estudios* (Madrid: Espasa-Calpe), 1976, pp. 7–93.

——, 1919, 1966. *Documentos lingüísticos de España, I. Reino de Castilla* (Madrid: CSIC).

——, 1923. 'Articulación lingüística de España', *Enciclopedia Espasa*, vol. XXI, s.v. 'España'. I refer to the separata with independent numbering: pp. 1–23.

——, 1926, 1950³. *Orígenes del español. Estado lingüístico de la Península Ibérica hasta el siglo XI* (Madrid: Espasa-Calpe).

——, 2005. *Historia de la lengua española*, 2 vols (Madrid: FRMP / RAE).

MORALA, José Ramón, ed., 2008. *Ramón Menéndez Pidal y 'El dialecto leonés' (1906–2006)* (León: Instituto Castellano y Leonés de la Lengua).

MORGADES, Josep, 2006. '(Con)textos d'un text: el del Primer Congrès de la Llengua', in *El Primer Congrés Internacional de la Llengua Catalana. Reflexos i projeccions*, ed. Maria Pilar Perea and Germà Colón Domènech (Barcelona / Castelló de la Plana: PPU), pp. 25–63.

NAVARRO TOMÁS, Tomás, [1919] 1957. *Documentos lingüísticos del Alto Aragón* (Syracuse, New York: University Press).

——, 1975. *Capítulos de geografía lingüística de la Península Ibérica* (Bogotá: Instituto Caro y Cuervo).

NEIRA MARTÍNEZ, Jesús, 1989. 'Las fronteras del leonés', in *Homenaje a Alonso Zamora Vicente*, vol. II (Madrid: Castalia), pp. 215–25.

PASCUAL RODRÍGUEZ, José Antonio, 1996–97. 'Variación fonética o norma gráfica en el español medieval. A propósito de los dialectos hispánicos centrales', *Cahiers de linguistique hispanique médiévále*, 21: 89–104.

——, 2004. 'Sobre la representación de los diptongos en la documentación medieval del monasterio de Sahagún y de la catedral de León', in *Orígenes de las lenguas romances en el reino de León. Siglos IX–XII*, vol. I (Léon: Centro de Estudios e Investigación San Isidoro / Caja España / Archivo Histórico Diocesano), pp. 501–31.

PASCUAL RODRÍGUEZ, José Antonio & Ramón SANTIAGO LACUESTA, 2003. 'Evolución fonética y tradiciones gráficas. Sobre la documentación del Monasterio de Sahagún en *Orígenes del español*', in *Lengua romance en textos latinos de la Edad Media*, ed. Hermógenes Perdiguero Villareal (Burgos: Universidad de Burgos / Instituto Castellano y Leonés de la Lengua), pp. 205–20.

PATO, Enrique, 2004a. *La sustitucion de 'cantara / cantase' por 'cantaría / cantaba' en el castellano septentrional peninsular* (Universidad Autónoma de Madrid / Ed. del autor) (http://www.ffil.uam.es/coser/publicaciones/enrique/2_es.pdf).

——, 2004b. 'Los perfectos fuertes analógicos en español', in *Actas del Congreso Internacional 'APLEx 2004'. Patrimonio Lingüístico Extremeño*, ed. M. Trinidad (Cáceres: Editora Regional) [ed. CD Rom]. English versión in: PATO, Enrique, 2009. 'Linguistic leveling in Spanish: The case of analogical strong preterits', *Canadian Journal of Linguistics*, 54 (to appear).

——, 2007. 'Sobre geografía léxica española: Distribución y áreas léxicas de la mustela'. Comunicación presentada en el *XXV Congrès International de Linguistique et de Philologie Romanes*. Innsbruck: Institut für Romanistik der Leopold-Franzens-Universität Innsbruck (3–8 de septiembre de 2007).

PENNY, Ralph, 2004a. *Variación y cambio en español* (Madrid: Gredos); English original, *Variation and Change in Spanish* (Cambridge: Cambridge University Press, 2000).

——, 2004b. 'Continuum dialectal y fronteras estatales: el caso del leonés medieval', in *Orígenes de las lenguas romances en el reino de León. Siglos IX–XII*, vol. I (León: Centro de Estudios e Investigación San Isidoro / Caja España / Archivo Histórico Diocesano), pp. 565–78.

PEREA, Maria Pilar, 2005. *Antoni M. Alcover. Dialectòleg, gramàtic, polemista* (Montcada i Reixac: Fundació Germà Colón Domènech / Publicacions de l'Abadia de Montserrat).

PÉREZ PASCUAL, José Ignacio, 1998. *Ramón Menéndez Pidal. Ciencia y pasión* (Valladolid: Conserjería de Educación y Cultura, Junta de Castilla y León).

PÉREZ VILLANUEVA, Joaquín, 1991. *Ramón Menéndez Pidal, su vida y su tiempo* (Madrid: Espasa-Calpe).

PORTOLÉS, José, 1986. *Medio siglo de filología española (1896–1952). Positivismo e idealismo* (Madrid: Cátedra).

RIDRUEJO, Emilio, 1995. 'Procesos migratorios y nivelación dialectal en los inicios de la reconquista castellana', in *Estudis de lingüística i filologia oferts a Antoni M. Badia i Margarit*, vol. II (Barcelona: Universitat de Barcelona / Publicacions de l'Abadia de Montserrat), pp. 235–48.

RODRÍGUEZ MOLINA, Javier, 2004. 'Difusión léxica, cambio semántico y gramaticalización: el caso de *haber* + participio en español antiguo', *RFE*, 84: 169–209.

——, 2008. 'La extraña sintaxis verbal del Libro de Alexandre', *Troianalexandrina*, 8: 115–46.

SANTANO MORENO, Julián, 2003. 'Menéndez Pidal y la filología del 98. Estado latente e intrahistoria', *Criticón*, 87–88–89: 787–98.

TUTEN, Donald N., 2003. *Koineization in Medieval Spanish* (Berlin / New York: Mouton de Gruyter).

UMPHREY, G. W., 1911. 'The Aragonese dialect', *Revue Hispanique*, 24: 5–45.

WRIGHT, Roger, 2000. *El Tratado de Cabreros (1206): estudio sociofilológico de una reforma ortográfica*. PMHRS, 19 (London: Department of Hispanic Studies, Queen Mary and Westfield College).

——, 2010. 'Ramón Menéndez Pidal and the History of the Spanish Language', in this volume.

Ramón Menéndez Pidal and the History of the Spanish Language

ROGER WRIGHT

(*University of Liverpool*)

One of the most remarkable publishing events of 2005 was the appearance of a new book by Ramón Menéndez Pidal, *Historia de la Lengua Española* (Madrid, RAE). This was not the delayed emergence of a minor intellectual sideline; it fills two large volumes, and 2,107 pages in all. It represents the culmination of over a century's worth of serious intentions. We can tell from comments he made when writing to Unamuno that Menéndez Pidal had already been planning to produce such a volume before he published his *Manual elemental de gramática histórica española* of 1904. The *Manual* of 1904, enlarged and much reprinted (since 1918, without the word *elemental* in the title), the two linguistic volumes of his edition of the *Cantar de Mio Cid* (1908, 1911: see Pérez Villanueva 1991: 222–23), and above all the astounding *Orígenes del Español* (1926), established the bases and set the scene for all of the study of the medieval development of the language ever since. The latter two are still essential for all scholars of Medieval Spanish to consult, despite the work of Yakov Malkiel and his academic descendants, and the Madison and CORDE materials (etc) that have been produced since; and any onlooker would feel that Menéndez Pidal had in no way failed subsequent researchers by not producing more. Menéndez Pidal himself did not feel that way, however; throughout the second half of his life his most serious academic plan for the future was to complete the proposed History of the Language volume, and even though outside events and other interests conspired to postpone this indefinitely, he considered that this was his most serious line of research enquiry. Shortly before his death, he told the journalist Carmen Conde, for example, who had no linguistic curiosity at all and so didn't follow this passing remark up, that he reckoned that the *Orígenes* was his most important work and the one which pleased him most (Conde 1969: 137). His grandson, the late Diego Catalán, knew that too;

Diego Catalán was not primarily by instinct a linguist, but he spent a long time carefully working out and collating the various drafts, published and unpublished, of what his grandfather had written towards the project, and thus was able to produce these two volumes almost forty years after their author's death. The second volume of the 2005 publication contains a prologue of seventy pages (pp. 7–75) written by Menéndez Pidal in 1939, followed by a lengthy account of the vicissitudes of all the chapter drafts and materials, of how they got moved from place to place in the Civil War, and of how Diego Catalán sorted out the text subsequently; which he achieved with remarkable acuity, seeing that the final result has its own internal coherence.

In the early 1940s, when he was effectively under house arrest in Madrid and hardly able to work on new projects at all, it was known among his friends and former students both that Menéndez Pidal had been long planning to write such a volume and that he was not in a position to complete it in the near future. In 1940 he produced a revised and extended version of the 1904 *Manual*. And then it was in 1942 that the first edition of Rafael Lapesa's *Historia de la Lengua Española* was published. In this, Menéndez Pidal's star student offered the public a work of the same title as his master had in mind, and understandably similar in inspiration and approach. Menéndez Pidal provided a brief laudatory prologue (also reproduced in later editions). Lapesa said in his own original preface that 'Mentor constante de mi trabajo han sido las obras de don Ramón Menéndez Pidal', although it is not clear how much of the content of Rafael Lapesa's work was inspired directly or indirectly by Menéndez Pidal himself at the time, for Menéndez Pidal's relationship with Lapesa's book is not covered in detail in Diego Catalán's account. It must have been more than nothing, and judging by the general manner of organization and approach to the material, Menéndez Pidal's contribution could have been a great deal. The approach of the two maestros was not identical, however. Lapesa saw more value in literary analyses, it seems, than Menéndez Pidal did. Lapesa devotes much of the space allotted in his book for the Castilian language from 1300 to the twentieth century essentially to a literary analysis of a sequence of great writers; a topic which most other historians of the Spanish Language, even within the Madrid tradition, have seen as largely unnecessary and no part of their brief. Lapesa extended this tendency even further in his 1980 revised version. Menéndez Pidal (2005) devotes some chapters to writers, but he concentrates on linguistic topics for the majority of his attention. As regards the years between 1554 and 1617, for example, Lapesa (1980) had one detailed chapter on 'El español del Siglo de Oro: la literatura barroca', including sections specifically on Cervantes, Lope de Vega, Góngora, Quevedo, Gracián and Calderón, followed by a chapter of similar length on 'El español del Siglo de Oro: cambios lingüísticos generales'. In comparison, Menéndez Pidal (2005) was able to focus on the language more directly, as only two of the six relevant chapters concentrate on literature:

Chapter 9   'Período de los grandes escritores místicos
              (1554–1585)'
Chapter 10   'Aspiración a una norma lingüística nacional'
Chapter 11   'Período de Cervantes y Lope de Vega (1585–1617)'
Chapter 12   'Estado de la lengua común (1550–1610)'
Chapter 13   'El desarrollo del andaluz y demás dialectos
              meridionales, 1557–1617'
Chapter 14   'Desarrollo del español en América'.

This relative concentration on linguistic matters represents an advance on Lapesa, but still seems an old-fashioned approach to linguistic history now, even so; in Spain as well as elsewhere. The chapter titles for that same period in the recent encyclopaedic *Historia de la Lengua Española*, the almost simultaneously produced volume of the same title containing the work of forty authors and edited by Lapesa's former student Rafael Cano in 2004, show clearly the general change in emphasis that there has been in Spain since Menéndez Pidal's day, as overall the contributors prefer to study the History of the Language through History, Texts and Linguistics, rather than via literature:

Chapter 26   'La España Moderna (1474–1700)'
Chapter 27   'La conciencia lingüística en la Edad de Oro'
Chapter 28   'Historia textual: textos literarios (Siglo de Oro)'
Chapter 29   'Textos entre inmediatez y distancia comunicativas:
              el problema de lo hablado escrito en el Siglo de Oro'

Menéndez Pidal's own enormous contribution to the field was and still is based on his work on early medieval data, and in particular on the *Orígenes del Español* of 1926. He was able to produce the slightly revised third edition of this in 1950. This has been also much reprinted, remains completely unsurpassed, and overshadows the work of all the other labourers in that early medieval garden. And it is possible that as well as being diverted in the late 1940s and 1950s by concerns that were of more immediate urgency in the heat of the moment, Menéndez Pidal realized, consciously or not, that Lapesa's handbook had largely filled the void which had inspired him to plan the large long-term project forty years before, and perhaps also that he himself did not have much more to say about many of the late medieval and Golden Age topics which Lapesa had already covered.

Lapesa was not the only former student to have overtaken him on the inside. The recently edited, and highly interesting, letters that Juan Corominas and Ramón Menéndez Pidal sent to each other, from 1939 until the mid-Sixties (Pascual and Pérez Pascual 2006), show that Menéndez Pidal was fully aware that in the light of Corominas's hugely energetic work rate he himself would not be able to become the pre-eminent figure in Hispanic etymology. Particularly after Corominas's move from Argentina to Chicago in 1947 it was clear to Menéndez Pidal, if not to Corominas, that Corominas had access in Chicago to more and better library facilities and materials, and graduate students, than he had himself in Madrid; and indeed, rather than seeing Corominas as any kind of rival, Menéndez Pidal did his best to help his former student. His assistance seems to have been eventually vital, for example, in getting the *Diccionario Crítico Etimológico de la Lengua Castellana* published in 1954, jointly by Gredos in Madrid and by Francke in Switzerland. Menéndez Pidal would have realized that for him to add significantly to the work of Lapesa and Corominas in the 1950s, when he was already old and feeling his age, and the other two were in any event constantly revising their own work, would have been difficult. Maybe, in the event, it is as well that the recently published material was not published before, because as it is now much of it does not really add to what we know. It would have been a useful book in 1960, of course. It is now a valuable source of data for any doctoral student working on Menéndez Pidal himself; but several sections are inevitably outdated, and it feels slightly sad that the publisher's and editor's sense of pietas has led them to believe that these collected chapters deserved priority de luxe treatment ahead of other monographs that had a chance of progressing the research area in the 21st century. That is, the appearance of this volume is in some part the effect, and perhaps also now a contributory cause, of a still persistent feeling that Menéndez Pidal had it all solved ages ago, such that any further research, or even ideas, about Early Medieval Spanish are unnecessary; an idea which a sesquicentenarian Menéndez Pidal alive today could not possibly have agreed with. When scholars in the field during the last forty years have disagreed with his perspective it is usually because they are, unsurprisingly, aware of advances and discoveries which Menéndez Pidal himself could not have been aware of, such as the development of sociolinguistics as an aid to philological research.

Yakov Malkiel (1970), who was not on the whole given to making generous assessments of his co-workers in the Iberian peninsula (including, noticeably, Corominas), said that when the *Orígenes del Español* came out in 1926 it temporarily put Spain into the vanguard of Romance Philological studies; and he was right. Both Spanish and foreign linguists of the time understandably looked on it with a sense of awe. Spanish scholars had not achieved any kind of prestige in the wider Romance field before then, and it was an awkward fact, which Menéndez Pidal was brave enough to face up to, that he needed to look outside the Peninsula for scholarly help in the study of this essential aspect of his own country's culture, in particular from the work of such German Romanist *éminences grises* as Diez, Meyer-Lübke and Baist. Yet Menéndez Pidal did not achieve his own eminent position by slavishly following the example or advice of any predecessors working on Romance areas, but from being to a large extent self-taught. In particular, as a part of his initial researches ultimately aimed towards preparing the Medieval section of a comprehensive *Historia de la Lengua*, he had found, by going out and looking for them in 1915, a large number of previously unstudied documents from tenth- and eleventh-century León in whose ostensibly Latin text there were several written features that he realized could reasonably be described as being features of Spanish rather than of Latin (if such a distinction had to be made at all). This is described in his conversations with Carmen Conde as being a kind of lightbulb moment: 'ese lenguaje notarial, bárbaramente iliterario en los siglos IX al XII, desatendido por los críticos completamente a causa de la tosquedad del mismo, me dio luz inesperada sobre muchos problemas lingüísticos' (Conde 1969: 36). This insight was an important discovery in itself, and his careful and lengthy analyses, mostly but not exclusively of the phonetic and inflectional realities which could be glimpsed underneath the Latinizing veneer of the documentation, are what have impressed all his readers since.

This overall concentration on phonetics and inflectional morphology had also been a feature of the *Manual*, although not of his studies on the *Cantar de Mio Cid* (whose two linguistic volumes were entitled *Gramática* and *Vocabulario*). A concentration on phonetics and inflectional morphology was also characteristic of many other Romance philological works of the first half of the twentieth century, but Menéndez Pidal's work is probably what has left it as the constantly most salient theme of most subsequent handbooks on the History of Spanish to this day. The late Paul Lloyd's *History of Spanish, Volume 1*, for example, is subtitled *Historical Phonology and Morphology of the Spanish Language* (1987), and will probably remain at that now, since the materials which he left on his death in December 2007 towards the second projected volume, on derivational morphology and syntax, are not likely to be amenable to subsequent expansion by his admirers into a posthumous volume such as Diego Catalán produced for his grandfather. Similarly, Ralph Penny's *A History of the Spanish Language* (1991; 2nd ed. 2002) devotes far less space to syntax, derivational morphology and semantic change than to phonetics and inflectional morphology. Indeed, it is only now, with the publication in progress of the cosmically-proportioned eight-volume *Sintaxis histórica de la lengua española* (beginning in 2006) edited by the indefatigable Concepción Company and her Mexican colleagues, that this imbalance is being righted, although on a lesser scale Rafael Cano has been doing valiant work on medieval Castilian syntax for years. Meanwhile, the absence of etymological, semantic and word-formation studies in Menéndez Pidal's main work was compensated for many years by the prodigious and idiosyncratic work of Yakov Malkiel, who may even have seen his work as complementary in this way to that of Don Ramón; a tradition which is still being continued valiantly by Steven Dworkin but by almost nobody else.

Another feature of Menéndez Pidal's work which has been much discussed recently concerns the ideological underpinning of an approach which instinctively assumes that the speech of Castile is more significant than that of any other area in the Peninsula, as recent analyses have noted the unfortunate consequences which this assumption has had and is still having (e.g. Inés Fernández-Ordóñez in this conference; Del Valle and Gabriel-Stheeman 2002; Gerli 2001; and also, thirty years earlier, Malkiel's academic obituary in *Romance Philology*, 23, 1970: 371–411). Hispanists interested in pursuing this aspect of his philological perspectives will find some mildly unfortunate comments in Menéndez Pidal's 1939 introduction as printed by Catalán. But the main point which is going to be made in the second half of the present presentation is a different one, and concerns the noun phrase which he chose for the title of the work, *Orígenes del Español*.

This choice of title has had an unintended and unfortunate consequence which he may in fact have glimpsed at the time and been intending to mitigate in his subsequent work. The sub-title of the book is *Estado lingüístico de la península ibérica hasta el siglo XI*, 'the linguistic state of the peninsula up to the eleventh century', with no indication in that phrase of when this period actually began; but the earliest documentation studied is from the second half of the tenth century, and as a result the period from then to 1100 has come to be known as the *época de orígenes*. Perhaps some of the first Spanish linguists to use that phrase with this chronological reference meant 'the period covered by the book *Orígenes del Español*'; but nowadays this phrase is more generally used to refer to precisely those centuries and no earlier. This phraseology has had the unfortunate additional consequence that some linguists, in Spain in particular, give the impression that they believe that the Spanish language 'originated' in those centuries in a linguistic rather than a merely textual sense. José María Saussol's book entitled *Ser y estar: orígenes de sus funciones en el Cantar de Mio Cid* (Sevilla 1977) is in fact rather a good one, but the title gives the impression that *ser* and *estar* didn't actually exist before they were used in that epic poem, and even seems to imply that nobody talked at all before then. But they did, and they did. The origins of the functions of *ser* and *estar* were brilliantly and thoroughly studied by Birte Stengaard, in fact, in 1991; the title of her study was *Vida y muerte de un campo semántico: un estudio de la evolución semántica de los verbos latinos 'stare', 'sedere' e 'iacere' del latín al romance del s.XIII*, and her analysis thus ends at roughly the same chronological point which Saussol regarded as the time of origin of the same development. Obviously, there was no chronological cut-off point before which people did not speak Spanish and after which they did speak Spanish, and Saussol would probably agree with this if we were to ask him; the composition of the *Cantar de Mio Cid*, whenever we think that was, did not have the concomitant effect that everybody went to bed the day before its composition speaking Latin and woke up the next day speaking a different language, the one which Menéndez Pidal somewhat anachronistically called *español* and which most Hispanists, referring to this period, now call *iberorromance*, or in English, Ibero-Romance (e.g. Wright 1995). There has always been continuity. This is indeed obvious, I hope, but some investigators act as if they do not believe it; as if the actual Spanish language began at that point, as opposed to its manifestation in reformed written literary form; what Christopher Pountain in his recent inaugural lecture referred to as 'the beginnings of Spanish / Castilian as an *Ausbau* language' (Pountain 2008). Partly they may have been misled by not appreciating the difference between linguistic change, which is continuous, and change in a language's name, which can be abrupt but need never happen at all, and when it does is quite a separate phenomenon from language change itself (cp. Janson 2002; Wright 2003, chapter 13).

It is good to be able to say that Menéndez Pidal himself was not misled by his own use of the phrase in the title of his book. He explains at the start (1926: vii), in a comment noted by Cravens (155) but probably not by every user of the volume, that 'no trataré ... los orígenes remotos de la lengua española, sino los orígenes próximos'. And in his most recent publication (2005), the only chapter or section heading to include the word *orígenes* is one where it has a sensible historical meaning, *Orígenes del reino de Navarra y del 'imperio' leonés* (Part 3, Chapter 4, Section 1, referring to the tenth century); the phrase *época de orígenes* only appears once (351) and *orígenes del español* not at all. The tenth and eleventh centuries are also referred to, reasonably, as 'esa época tan tenebrosa' (350), and, less reasonably, as 'el período arcaico' (347); this is less reasonable in that every period seems archaic to those more interested in later times, but this age does not seem at all archaic to scholars who work on the Visigothic texts. The pages on this period in the new publication are said by Catalán to have been a revision of *Orígenes*, made in 1947, but they are considerably less than that; they are in essence a more readable but much shorter and less academically intensive summary of the main points of the original *Orígenes*, with no noticeable updating of thoughts, bibliographical references or data since 1939, and hardly any since 1926.

He does seem to let himself down rather, though, with the extraordinary chapter title (Part 3, Chapter 5) *Primeros balbuceos del idioma 960–1065; glosas y cantares épicos*, which is so uncharacteristically misconceived that it is possible to suspect that it may come from Diego Catalán rather than from Menéndez Pidal himself; the sections in this chapter are noticeably more careful than that title is to distinguish between speech, which is what *balbuceos* refer to, and revolutionary writing, which is what the Riojan glosses and the text of the *Poema de Mio Cid* attest. There are, unfortunately, a few detailed comments in which Menéndez Pidal does seem unhelpfully to confuse letters and sounds, such as: 'El sonido *ce, ci* y *z* africada dental, sorda y sonora respectivamente' (331; in which *ce, ci* and *z* are letters, not sounds); but none of them are as seriously misleading as the title given to the chapter as a whole. Indeed, the initial two sentences of the new chapter are as follows: 'Sería no sólo arbitrario sino muy impropio querer fijar una fecha del nacimiento del romance, pues su evolución distintiva del latín clásico comienza en la época romana y continúa ininterrumpidamente en los siglos siguientes. Pero sí podemos decir que en el siglo X nace la nueva lengua escrita' (319); this perspective represented an advance at the time it was written, and is still a valuable comment, even though modern scholarship has established the date of the Riojan Glosses to be of the following century; and we could add that what was 'born' with them was not so much a new language as a new way of writing the existing language. But if we took this chapter title seriously, as a summary of what Menéndez Pidal in 1939 thought of the language of those years, thereby negating the thoughtful analyses of his 1926 work in which he considers carefully what the scribes were actually saying, we would need to come to the improbable conclusion that he thought that nobody could talk their own language coherently in those years and that everybody was reduced to a kind of stammering (*balbuceos*). There have been scholars who seriously believed this absurdity; Gregorio Salvador seemed at one point in the 1980s to be suggesting that nobody could talk at all in the Early Middle Ages (Salvador 1988: 645); but as Alarcos Llorach pointed out in 1982, whatever linguists mean by this kind of remark they cannot mean that people were unable to talk sensibly at all, and their everyday language served them as well then as everybody's spoken vernacular always does at any time (see also Wright 2004a). It would be best to avoid all these metaphors of discontinuity, including the one about the Glosses representing the 'birth' of Spanish which is often derided these days, but often implicitly accepted even so. Even Menéndez Pidal himself got carried away with this metaphor when summarizing the eleventh-century documentation, both in 1926 and later: the section in the new publication concludes by telling us that "dentro del cuerpo de la lengua escrita se agita y remueve embrionaria la frase romance, como criatura que empieza a vivir dentro del claustro materno que le da el ser" (323), which is a phrase taken from a larger extended metaphor in the conclusions of the *Orígenes* (paragraph 111.3)

In fact, of course, everybody could and can always talk their own native vernacular, whatever we think the name of their language was or should have been. Any attempt to fix a starting point for the history or the origins of the Spanish Language, or for any language other than a genuinely creolized pidgin, is necessarily artificial. In practice, the commonest place for beginning the History of Spanish in the most commonly used University handbooks is not 960 A.D. (as in the title given to these pages in Menéndez Pidal 2005) but with the Roman invasions of the end of the third century B.C. Ralph Penny starts his chronological timeline there, and Paul Lloyd opens his account with the Latin of the Roman Empire. This perspective is surely preferable to seeing the origins of the language itself (as opposed to the origins of its distinguishable textual attestations) in the tenth century. And recent sociolinguistic advances have reinforced the instinct commonly felt by historians of the Spanish Language, that they should start their account from the date of the arrival of the Romans, rather than from any earlier time; although this late third-century B.C. date is of no great significance from an internal linguistic point of view, the permanent arrival of Romans speaking a variety of different Latin dialects in the Eastern Peninsula is likely to have been followed by a sociolinguistically significant period crucial to the development of some of the emigrant features which were to lead eventually to Iberian Romance (although, as Jim Adams observes in his recent 2006 book, there is no surviving detailed evidence for this process). The point is that recent advances in the analysis of the development of colonial dialects, out of a mix of mutually comprehensible but different contributory dialects, show that there is usually a sociolinguistic turning-point in the two or three generations following the initial colonization; that is, during the period from about 180 B.C. until about 130 B.C. the descendants of the original Latin-speaking settlers in the Peninsula are quite likely to have developed something of an emigrant dialect on the East Coast on the pattern which has been so brilliantly described for New Zealand English by Peter Trudgill (2004). But even given this sophisticated reassessment of which periods are likely to have been sociolinguistically significant, the history of the language in strictly linguistic terms descends in an unbroken line of descent from the Proto-Indo-European of 3,500 B.C., and indeed from many thousands of years before that, and when linguists use the word "origins" in connection with language history, they are usually phenomena in the far distant prehistoric past that they are considering: what Henriette Walter (1994: 25) calls "les origines lointaines" of modern Indo-European languages, for example, are, in her account, the features of Indo-European itself.

Those who work on the history of other areas of Romance have a different chronological perspective about origins. Scholars working on the history of Italian, such as Ernst Pulgram, for example, naturally envisage no such turning point at the time of the second Punic War in the late third century B.C.; and so several of the contributors to the volume of essays entitled *La preistoria dell'italiano*, which József Herman and Anna Marinetti edited in 2000, wrote on pre-Roman developments. Being mainly a Hispanist, it never occurred to me to write on any topic so early (my own piece in that volume is on the eighth century A.D.). Even so, not all Romanists in Italy share this perspective; some have also used the word Origini in book titles in less than satisfactory ways, such as Tagliavini (1972), who was explicitly considering the new written languages in his *Origini delle lingue neolatine* (cp. Cravens 2007: 156). And some of the French scholars now writing on the History of French are even more chronologically adventurous than Pulgram; Michèle Perret's *Introduction a l'histoire de la langue française* of 1998, for example, is highly recommendable and not very long, but starts with a chapter entitled *Les origines: les familles de langues*, which itself begins with precisely the question 'Peut-on connaître l'origine des langues?', and devotes several pages to Indo-European as the 'origine commune' of so many modern languages, including a section on the ideas of Colin Renfrew concerning agriculture and the diffusion of Indo-European eight thousand years ago, which in turn leads up to a section (p.19) considering the possibility of going even further back to what has come to be called 'Nostratic'. This chapter surprised me when I saw it, given that this book is an introductory handbook on the history of French, but it is worth remembering that French linguists have proved to be particularly intrigued by the possibility of reconstructing 'Proto-World'. This is all discussed by Michèle Perret before she considers the nature of Latin at all, let alone Romance. But perhaps the most remarkable recent example of the realization that there is a seamless history from Indo-European to all its modern descendants comes in the first volume of the currently appearing multi-volumed OUP series entitled *History of the English Language*. This first volume chronologically is by Don Ringe (2006), and is entitled *From Proto-Indo-European to Proto-Germanic*; that is, this solid book on the History of English actually ends long before the language even approaches these shores.

In its way, this is all most encouraging. And I am certainly not saying that Menéndez Pidal should have written two chapters on Proto-Indo-European in his 1926 work. I am just suggesting that it was unfortunate that he should have used the word *Orígenes* in the title of a book which concentrated on the Spanish of the tenth and eleventh centuries, which is really a relatively recent period in its overall history. In the event it seems highly likely that Menéndez Pidal, in his linguistic investigations during and after the Civil War, realized a need to extend his chronological expertise backwards in time. The evidence for this is that in Paris in 1938 he was working on pre-Roman toponymy; then when he first reapproached the long-term *Historia de la Lengua* project in the 1940s, he decided to spend some of his academic energy investigating that pre-Roman period, as is now evident in the first part of his recent publication. In his case, however, it seems that his instincts and motives were not those of Pulgram or the other linguists who have perceived the unhelpfulness of linguistic periodizations based on the progressive expansion of the Roman Empire, since he shows no direct interest in investigating the older stages of the language he is ostensibly studying, that is, those which are usually called Early Latin or Italic or Indo-European. Menéndez Pidal's instincts at that point were those of a nationalist historian of the Franco era, since he decided instead to study the pre-Roman languages of the Iberian Peninsula, which now fill the first eighty-odd pages of the new book. This is a most interesting topic in itself, of course, although his account is now out of date in that so much more is known about these in 2008 than was known in the 1940s, but it is of limited value to the ostensible theme of the work as a whole, since apart from toponymy this research is of marginal relevance to the "History of the Spanish Language". But at least he accepted in the late 1940s that the History of Spanish had not in fact begun in the tenth century A.D. Yet even after these copious earlier investigations, he was still inclined to refer to the tenth century as the "período de los orígenes románicos", even when making an excellent point: that the Leonese documents of the time "nos permiten insistir sobre lo inconveniente que es establecer un divorcio entre la lengua hablada y el latín escrito en el período de los orígenes románicos" (321).

As Tom Cravens (2007) has recently pointed out, though, the word may have misled many generations of students of the History of the

Spanish Language, and several researchers, into thinking that data from before the mid-tenth century A.D. are no part of their brief. In Spain this potential misunderstanding has been abetted by the reluctance or sometimes the inability of Hispanists and Latinists to meet and talk to each other, or even be interested in what they see as the others' field, leading to suspicions at high levels and a feeling that since the University Departments of Latin and of Hispanic Studies are usually administratively different, all the subject matter must be different as well (cp. Wright 2004b).

Surprisingly, and worryingly, one of those scholars apparently misled by the maestro's use of the word *orígenes* was the late Juan Corominas himself. This is a problematic aspect of his Etymological Dictionaries which it is advisable to warn students about, although nobody has yet pointed this out in print. The problem is this. In each entry in the Etymological Dictionaries, Corominas wants to give his readers a date for the word's first attestation. In cases of borrowings from other languages, and of forms newly derived through the use of affixes, this information is potentially accessible, and helpful to subsequent researchers, although the precise datings given by Corominas have often been pushed back since by the subsequent dwarves who have stood on the giant's shoulders. But for Spanish words which have uncontroversially derived directly from spoken Latin, of which there are naturally a huge number, this practice of offering a date for the first attestation can be confusing. Bear in mind that the Historians of the Language now tend to start their field of operations around the year 200 B.C.; this implies that if the word in question existed in or before the second century B.C., and was attested then, then that (or earlier) is the period of the word's first attestation; but Corominas does not want to look earlier than the so-called *época de orígenes*, and is liable to tell us that such a word is attested from the *orígenes de la lengua* and give us an eleventh or twelfth-century attestation as its *primera documentación*.

Sometimes what Corominas does is to give us the first example he knows of in what was to be later the usual Romance spelling, as in: 'TORO, del lat. TAURUS íd. *1.ª doc.*: doc. de 1102, Oeschl.; Berceo' (Corominas 1954); or the first example he knows of in a non-Latin spelling, even if the eventual Castilian form was going to be different, as in: 'TÓRTOLA, del lat. TŬRTUR, -ŬRIS , íd. *1.ª doc.*: tórtora,

Berceo, *Sacrif.*, 7, 21'. Some words are so common that he just tells us that the word is there in the origins of the language, by which he explicitly means the period analysed in Menéndez Pidal's *Orígenes*; consider, for example, the apparent implications of the start of the entry for todo: 'TODO, del lat. TŌTUS 'todo entero'. *1.ª doc.*: orígenes (Glosas Emilianenses y Silenses, *Cid*, etc.).'. From these entries an unwarned reader would never guess that the word (as supposed to the accident of its most recent orthographical manifestation) had existed for a thousand years and more before the period mentioned. At least in the case of *toro*, *tórtola* and *todo* there has been some slight phonetic development (although undoubtedly starting long before the time of the *Glosas Emilianenses*), which led in due course to a graphical change, which might be the excuse for Corominas's apparent indication that each of these was a new word rather than an old word with a new written form; in some cases in which there has been no semantic development, and minimal or no phonetic evolution, and as a result not even the spelling has ever changed, it is unclear why Corominas has chosen the attestation which he has rather than admitting that the same word had already been there for centuries before this so-called age of *orígenes*. An example of this confusion is at the start of the entry for the word *tanto*; this word has existed since Roman times and before, with essentially the same meaning as it still has now, but even so the entry in Corominas's dictionary begins as follows: 'TANTO, del lat. TANTUS, -A, -UM , 'tan grande'. *1.ª doc.*: orígenes (*Cid*, etc.).' Any linguist at all can point to earlier attestations of *tanto* than those of the *Poema de Mio Cid* just by looking in a dictionary: Plautus used it, for example, fourteen centuries before.

Astonishing though Corominas's general achievements are, it seems that having been Menéndez Pidal's doctoral student in the 1930s he had too much instinctive respect for his master in the 1940s and 1950s to realize that his adoption of the term has led his chronological indications of initial attestations in such cases to risk being seriously misleading. This desire to avoid mentioning earlier attestations does not arise from Corominas not knowing evidence from earlier times, because he does; he tells us a great deal, in some of the lengthy discussions, about texts of the Roman Empire, and also from time to time about Indo-European scholarship and cognate words. He also makes some valuable references to Peninsular texts from the period before that of these supposed origins; his discussion of the Spanish word *tío*, for example, which was a borrowing from Early Medieval Greek, refers as it should to Isidore of Seville, who used it at the start of the seventh century in a passage which probably really is the first written attestation of the word in the language in the Peninsula. And yet, despite his knowledge of the appearance of the word in the works of Isidore, Corominas's entry had begun as follows: 'TÍO y TÍA, del latín tardío THĪUS, THĪA , y éstos del gr. θεῖος, θεία, íd. *1.ª doc.*: 2.ª mitad S. X, Glosas Silenses', three centuries later than the documentation which he then goes on to mention.

Anyway, it is time to come to some kind of a conclusion. On the whole, indisputably, Menéndez Pidal's work on the History of the Spanish Language was superb, the result of acute insight and determined hard work. The *Orígenes del español* is rightly admired and necessarily consulted, even eighty years afterwards. The general reflections on the nature of language variation and change, and in particular of phonetic change, which he included at the end of the book, seem more pertinent now than they could have done in 1926, when the neogrammarian paradigm was still in vogue. Indeed, the credit for the current healthy state of the academic study of the History of the Spanish Language in Spain can ultimately be attributed to Menéndez Pidal. The triennial conferences on the History of the Spanish Language in Spain regularly attract up to a thousand attenders, the Acts regularly run to two thousand pages, and the quality is often high although rarely adventurous. The study of the History of the Spanish Language is still an integral part of undergraduate courses more often in Spain than it is in the USA or in Britain; and the presence of so many excellent researchers from Spain in the International Romanística conferences becomes more salient each time they are held. Menéndez Pidal's academic pupils, and then their pupils, have set a standard for careful and detailed philological analysis which still deserves all our admiration. Inés Fernández Ordóñez is one of the very best examples of these; she wrote an outstanding chapter on thirteenth-century Castilian in the encyclopaedia edited by Rafael Cano, for example; but she is not alone. Menéndez Pidal set a trend which continues to this day, and which is still overwhelmingly positive in most of its effects, despite the criticisms which can be made, from a later vantage point, of some of his assumptions.

Works Cited

Adams, J. N., 2006. *The Regional Diversification of Latin, 200 B. C. – A. D. 600* (Oxford: Oxford UP).

Alarcos Llorach, Emilio, 1982. *El español, lengua milenaria* (Valladolid: Ámbito).

Cano, Rafael, ed., 2004. *Historia de la lengua española* (Barcelona: Ariel).

Company Company, Concepción, ed., 2006. *Sintaxis histórica de la lengua española*, vols 1 and 2 (Mexico: UNAM).

Conde, Carmen, 1969. *Menéndez Pidal* (Madrid: Unión).

Corominas, Juan, 1954. *Diccionario crítico etimológico de la lengua castellana* (Madrid: Gredos; Berne: Francke).

Cravens, Thomas D., 2007. 'Perils of speaking of Orígenes de la lengua', in *Medieval Iberia: changing societies and cultures in contact and transition*, ed. Ivy A. Corfis and Ray Harris-Northall (Woodbridge: Tamesis), pp. 153–64.

Del Valle, José and Luis Gabriel-Stheeman, ed., 2002. *The Battle over Spanish between 1800 and 2000: Language Ideologies and Hispanic Intellectuals* (London: Routledge).

Fernández-Ordóñez, Inés, 2004. 'Alfonso X el Sabio en la historia del español', in Cano (ed., 2004), pp. 381–422.

Gerli, E. Michael, 2001. 'Inventing the Spanish Middle Ages: Ramón Menéndez Pidal, Spanish cultural history, and ideology in philology', *C*, 30.1: 111–26.

Herman, József and Anna Marinetti, ed., 2000. *La preistoria dell'italiano* (Tübingen: Niemeyer).

Hess, Steven, 1982. *Ramón Menéndez Pidal* (Boston: Twayne).

Janson, Tore, 2002. *Speak: a Short History of Languages* (Oxford: Oxford UP).

Lapesa, Rafael, 1942 (8th ed. 1980). *Historia de la lengua española* (Madrid: Gredos).

Lloyd, Paul, 1987. *From Latin to Spanish, Vol. I: Historical Phonology and Morphology of the Spanish Language* (Philadelphia: American Philosophical Society).

Malkiel, Yakov, 1970. 'Era omne esencial ...', *RPh*, 23: 371–411.

Menéndez Pidal, Ramón, 1904 (and much reprinted; since the fourth ed. of 1918, without the *elemental*). *Manual elemental de gramática histórica española* (Madrid: Espasa-Calpe).

——, 1908/1911. *Cantar de Mio Cid: texto, gramática y vocabulario*; vol. II, *Vocabulario*; vol. III, *Gramática* (Madrid: Espasa-Calpe).

——, 2005. *Historia de la lengua española* (Madrid: RAE).

PASCUAL, José Antonio and José Ignacio PÉREZ PASCUAL, 2006. *Epistolario Joan Coromines & Ramón Menéndez Pidal* (Barcelona: Fundació Pere Coromines).

PENNY, Ralph, 1991 (2nd ed., 2002). *A History of the Spanish Language* (Cambridge: Cambridge UP).

PÉREZ VILLANUEVA, Joaquín, 1991. *Ramón Menéndez Pidal: su vida y su tiempo* (Madrid: Espasa-Calpe).

PERRET, Michèle, 1998. *Introduction à l'histoire de la langue française* (Paris: Sedes).

POUNTAIN, Christopher, 2008. 'Putting philology back into linguistics'. Inaugural lecture delivered at Queen Mary, London.

PULGRAM, Ernst, 1978. *Italic, Latin, Italian: 600 B.C. to A.D. 1260* (Heidelberg: Winter).

RINGE, Don, 2006. *History of the English Language vol. I: From Proto-Indo-European to Proto-Germanic* (Oxford: Oxford UP).

SALVADOR, Gregorio, 1988. 'Lexemática histórica', in *Actas del I Congreso Internacional de Historia de la Lengua Española*, ed. Manuel Ariza et al. (Madrid: Arco Libros), pp. 635–46.

SAUSSOL, José María, 1977. *Ser y estar: orígenes de sus funciones en el Cantar de Mio Cid* (Sevilla: Universidad de Sevilla).

STENGAARD, Birte, 1991. *Vida y muerte de un campo semántico: un estudio de la evolución semántica de los verbos latinos 'stare', 'sedere' e 'iacere' del latín al romance del s.XIII* (Tübingen: Niemeyer).

TAGLIAVINI, Carlo, 1972. *Le origini delle lingue neolatine*, 6th ed. (Bologna: Pàtron).

TRUDGILL, Peter, 2004. *New-Dialect Formation: the Inevitability of Colonial Englishes* (Edinburgh: Edinburgh UP).

WALTER, Henriette, 1994. *L'aventure des langues en occident* (Paris: Robert Lafont).

WRIGHT, Roger, 1995. *Early Ibero-Romance: Twenty-one Studies on Language and Texts from the Iberian Peninsula between the Roman Empire and the Thirteenth Century* (Newark, DE: Juan de la Cuesta).

——, 2003. *A Sociophilological Study of Late Latin* (Turnhout: Brepols).

——, 2004a. 'El romance: nuevo sistema, o nueva colección de rasgos?', *Aemilianense*, 1: 665–87; www.vallenajerilla.com/berceo/rwright/romance.htm.

——, 2004b. 'Latinistas tardíos y romanistas tempranos', *Signo*, 14: 7–26.

Index of Scholars and Subjects